Cooperative Housing and Community Development

Donald G. Sullivan

The Praeger Special Studies program—
utilizing the most modern and efficient book
production techniques and a selective
worldwide distribution network—makes
available to the academic, government, and
business communities significant, timely
research in U.S. and international economic, social, and political development.

Cooperative Housing and Community Development

A Comparative Evaluation of Three Housing Projects in East Harlem

PRAEGER SPECIAL STUDIES IN U.S. ECONOMIC AND SOCIAL DEVELOPMENT

Praeger Publishers   New York   Washington   London

PRAEGER PUBLISHERS
111 Fourth Avenue, New York, N.Y. 10003, U.S.A.
5, Cromwell Place, London S.W.7, England

Published in the United States of America in 1971
by Praeger Publishers, Inc.

Library of Congress Catalog Card Number: 74-149283

Printed in the United States of America

The author wishes to express his sincere appreciation to the many people who have contributed their help and support to this study.

The graduate committee--Professor Lewis L. Bower, chairman; Professor Allan G. Feldt; and Professor Glenn H. Beyer--were most generous in their advise, constructive recommendations and support.

For the financial assistance necessary to carry out this study the author is indebted to the Family and Community Teams (FACT) Committee of Cornell University, especially to Mrs. Sylvia G. Wahl, whose invaluable encouragement and guidance made this study a reality. The author is grateful to Professor Ethel G. Vatter and the members of the FACT Committee for their support and to Professor Joseph Carreiro, Head of the Department of Housing and Design, for allocating additional funding to complete this study.

The interest and cooperation of Mrs. Ruth Senior, Association for Middle-Income Housing; Harry Fialkin, Chief of Statistics, New York City Housing Authority; and Frank Kristof, New York City Housing and Development Administration were invaluable. Miss Barbara Selwyn, as research assistant in the initial collection of data, was enthusiastic and a source of great encouragement throughout the study. The Lee Andrews Research firm rendered invaluable advice in the collection of data, and their expertise was most beneficial. Edward Morse and John Kimberly provided their knowledge in the statistical analysis of data. The use of the computer was greatly facilitated by the work of Perry Odak and by Professor Earl Morris, Department of Housing and Design, who offered their professional expertise, as well as advice and encouragement from the inception of this study. Finally, thanks are due to my colleagues at Hunter College who encouraged me to publish this study. The assistance of Mark Hinshaw in revising parts of the study was invaluable.

CONTENTS

LIST OF TABLES

Cooperative Housing and Community Development

EAST HARLEM

1 LEXINGTON HOUSES
2 JEFFERSON HOUSES
3 FRANKLIN PLAZA

N

The revitalization and redevelopment of the central city is the most important domestic challenge faced by public policy makers today. In spite of a large number of programs attempting to meet this challenge, results have been far from successful in creating the type of living environment deemed satisfactory for the urban dweller. This is especially true for low- and moderate-income level families, who are not afforded the option of competing effectively in the urban housing market.

In the search for workable programs to develop the residential areas where these families live, housing policy, primarily in the form of public housing, has received a major emphasis and, in many cases, a disproportionate emphasis, as a solution to the complex problems facing these families. The criticisms levied against the public housing program are numerous and, in many instances, justified. Since the physical improvement of housing conditions is not sufficient in itself, alternatives to existing housing policy must be developed that incorporate more important social goals related to individual and community development. The incorporation of such goals into national housing policy is beginning to gain impetus but is far from adequate.[1]

The belief that cooperative tenure will provide a means of achieving these goals has been proposed by a growing number of professionals and policy makers. This belief is largely founded on the premise that the existing rental tenure policy prescribed for public housing tenants is not related to community development. Acknowledging the need for alternative strategies, this study seeks to examine the associations, if any, between certain social phenomena and tenure. It seeks further to test certain hypotheses as to various presumed relationships associated with cooperative tenure and rental tenure. This study is motivated by a concern for housing policy, particularly that which seeks to employ the use of cooperative tenure for the social well-being of low- and moderate-income families. In view of the current emphasis on cooperative tenure and the assumptions made regarding its social effects, this study aims at providing empirically based research in a subject area that is currently void of such research.

The application of exacting methods of inquiry to the subject of cooperative tenure and its related social effects is a challenging and important task. A scientific approach to analysis and policy development is no less unique in housing than in other fields of study.[2] The literature on cooperative tenure is filled with hunches, intuitions, assumptions and subjective impressions, many of which can and should be explored more carefully through scientific investigation. The outstanding need in this subject area is an impartial examination of a set of primary propositions or hypotheses based on the claims made regarding the social effects of cooperative tenure.* This need was recognized as a field of research deserving support by the Family and Community Teams (FACT) Committee of Cornell University, an action-oriented research group, organized to encourage policy studies of social factors affecting the lives

---

*The social "effects" in question pertain to such aspects of the residential community as neighborly interaction, participation in community affairs, community solidarity and attitudes and feelings regarding housing, including pride in residence.

of urban residents. The assistance offered by the
FACT Committee allowed for this empirical analysis
of the tenure variable, based on field interviews in
the East Harlem community.

A review of current housing policy clearly
indicates a focus on programs related to the broad
goal of community development.* The concern of
housing professionals for programs oriented toward
community development is largely influenced by a
vast body of research and theoretical work that is
concerned with the decline of the community in an
industrialized, urban nation.[3] It has been stated
that the disintegration of community is considered
to be one of the most serious results of the rapid
urbanization and industrialization of modern society.
Ralph Linton makes the point that this phenomenon
has occurred so rapidly that the average adult is
still a person who was conditioned in childhood to
life on a community-oriented basis.[4]

It must be noted that a great deal of ambiguity
and uncertainty accompanies the popularizing of the
community development objective in housing policy
formulation. The theoretical literature relating to
high-density urban areas, particularly for the vertical residential districts characterizing the low-
income neighborhoods of large American cities, leaves
much to be desired in terms of policy strategies.
Indeed, the accusation made regarding the folklore

----

*There is no single or precise definition of
community or the functions of the community. One of
the most meaningful definitions of the term is provided by Albert J. Reiss, Jr., in "The Sociological
Study of Communities," Rural Sociology, XXIV, No. 2
(June, 1959), 118. Reiss states: "A community arises
through sharing a limited territorial space for
residence and for sustenance and functions to meet
common needs generated in sharing this space by establishing characteristic forms of social action."

of cooperative tenure can be applied to many of the
assumptions postulated regarding the factors associated with the processes of community development.
In both cases, however, these shortcomings have not
deterred many policy makers from effectuating housing
programs that rely more heavily on untested assumptions
than empirically based evidence. The dangers of such
action should be more than evident to any contemporary
analyst of this nation's experience with publicly
assisted housing.[5] The harsh reality of public
opinion regarding government intervention into the
sacred domain of the housing market should cause
those associated with the field to be especially wary
of justifying programs on social factors that may not
be founded in reality. The history of the public
housing program and the arguments posed regarding the
presumed association between changes in behavior and
housing conditions would be one example of policy
relying, in part, on claims that a host of eager
critics were quick to indict on the basis that the
program was not bringing about the results that it
was supposed to engender.

In view of the popularity of current proposals
related to cooperative tenure and its presumed social
effects for low- and moderate-income residents, it is
important to clarify the myths and realities of this
important area of housing. Accepting the need for
reevaluation of rental tenure policy in publicly
assisted housing, as well as the scientific testing
of the social benefits claimed for cooperative tenure,
this study incorporates some of the fundamental
factors associated with the term "community development" in establishing the conceptual guidelines for
its framework of analysis. Three housing developments
in New York City's East Harlem provide the study
setting: one being a moderate-income cooperative;
the second, a moderate-income public rental project;
and the third, a low-income public rental project.
These are described in detail later in this study.
The evaluation of selected social phenomena, related
to concepts of community development, provides the
focus for this study and the basis for the establishment of testable hypotheses.

This study rests on the proposition that the underlying philosophy of cooperative housing challenges the ability of the housing profession to find solutions to urgent problems facing urban dwellers. Underscoring this challenge, the statement has been made that housing is seen by professionals "as a fulcrum at which desirable changes in people's lives can be initiated."[6] If, indeed, housing policy, and, specifically, cooperative tenure policy, can facilitate important social goals, there is, then, a need for evaluative empirical research to guide the development of housing policy.

NOTES

1. In introducing Title 1 of the Demonstration Cities and Metropolitan Development Act of 1966, President Lyndon B. Johnson stated that the major goal of this Act is "to build not just housing units, but neighborhoods."

2. The most cogent arguments made for the employment of scientific methodology in housing research are found in Robert K. Merton, "The Social Psychology of Housing," in Wayne Dennis, ed., Current Trends in Social Psychology (Pittsburgh: University of Pittsburgh Press, 1948), pp. 163-217.

3. A definitive study of the disintegration of the community is provided in Robert Nisbet's The Quest for Community (New York: Oxford University Press, 1953).

4. Ralph Linton, The Study of Man (New York: Appleton-Century-Crofts, 1936), pp. 229-30.

5. A thorough analysis of the politics involving public housing is found in Leonard Freedman, Public Housing: The Politics of Poverty (Holt, Rinehart and Winston, 1969).

6. Kurt W. Back, Slums, Projects and People (Durham, N.C.: Duke University Press, 1962), p. 4.

2

THE SOCIAL EFFECTS
OF COOPERATIVE TENURE:
A REVIEW
OF THE LITERATURE

The research needs of the field of housing are many and diverse. Factual data relating to every aspect of housing need to be accumulated, analyzed and interpreted. This is particularly important for the relatively new policy of advocating cooperative tenure for public housing tenants and low-income slum dwellers, in that this policy rests on untested theoretical concepts of social phenomena related to the cooperative form of ownership. There has been little research that attempts to develop a descriptive theory of the social structure of a cooperatively owned residential community.

The literature reviewed in this chapter will be highly selective; an effort will be made to choose only those works that represent the main points of view concerning the major assumptions of the social effects of cooperative housing.*

_____

*This limitation is imposed because there have been no serious empirical studies that have scientifically proven or disproven the assumptions found throughout the literature. An exhaustive review of these assumptions would not contribute to explaining the data presented in this study.

From this literature emerge two central ideas
concerning cooperative tenure. The first is that
this form of tenure is related to numerous positive
social effects; the second, that the social failures
of public housing have been associated, in part, with
the rental tenure policy that prevails. These ideas,
also, may be seen in the historical development of
the legislation that has promoted cooperative tenure,
in that they have been incorporated as an underlying
rationale for the encouragement of this form of
housing. The connection between theory and actual
tenure policy in the public housing program cannot
be overlooked; therefore, the historical development
of housing tenure policy will also be examined in
this chapter.

TENURE POLICY IN PUBLIC HOUSING

Early in the development of the Federal Public
Housing program, rental policy seems to have been
accepted, because it was felt that those eligible
for government-subsidized housing lacked the job
security or "savings habit" that was necessary for
responsible home ownership. The usual apartment
projects were considered unsuitable for ownership,
in that they were multiple-dwelling buildings.
Little was known of the cooperative plan of ownership,
and New York City was the only city in the nation that
had utilized cooperatives to any significant extent
as an alternative to either single-family homes or
rental units. The still uneasy economic situation
of the Depression and the emphasis placed on the
economic and physical role of housing rather than its
social role were additional factors behind the original
decisions made in the early years of housing legislation. Added to these reasons is the rigidity with
which "home ownership" has been defined and viewed,
an outlook that seemed to allow no intermediary form
between single-family home ownership and the rental
of apartment units.

Following World War II, the discussion of tenure
policy began to appear in the literature on publicly
subsidized housing. In the short period of its

existence, public housing had gained more critics
than proponents. The social failures of public
housing have been well documented by a host of professionals concerned with housing. To review these
criticisms would be impossible within the limits of
this study.[1] The failures documented center largely
upon the drab and institutional quality of life that
is created in projects. Public housing projects
seem to remain merely "projects," failing to evoke
any sort of community feeling. Instead of setting
an example of better family and neighborhood living,
they develop, according to the critics, into sterile,
segregated enclaves, lacking in the variety and interaction that should be the prime features of a viable
residential community. Coupled with the belief that
public housing contributes to feelings of social
insecurity and lack of pride in one's home, it is
small wonder that alternatives to the program have
been proposed.

The writings of Catherine Bauer Wurster, one of
the most articulate analysts of the public housing
program, contain one of the earliest references
suggesting cooperative tenure for public housing.[2]
Although she questions the generally accepted goal
of ownership as being a carry-over from a romanti-
cized notion of the American past, she urges that
forms of cooperative housing be studied as alternatives
to rental tenure in public housing. In reviewing the
range of alternatives to public housing, Beyer men-
tions housing cooperatives but makes the point that
"it is questionable whether large groups of low-income
families could ever be accommodated."[3] Cooperative
tenure was cited as a means of dealing with a perplex-
ing issue facing the public housing program by Robert
M. Fisher in his book reviewing the economic aspects
of public housing. In discussing the subject of rent
levels, Fisher stated that "recent proposals to sell
public-housing units to over-income tenants on a
cooperative basis represent an attempt to deal with
this dilemma."[4]

By the early sixties, interest in tenure policy was
receiving considerable emphasis, as criticism against
public housing mounted. Ernest M. Fisher wrote in

his work on housing policy that "some public housing units should be made available for cooperative ownership or rental, or directly for sale."[5] National housing organizations followed this trend, and tenure policy was included in testimonies prepared for Congress. In a statement of the National Housing Conference, Nathaniel S. Keith recommended

> authorization for the sale of projects or
> parts thereof to tenant cooperatives or
> to tenants where they are prepared for
> home ownership responsibility, and where
> such sale would serve local housing needs
> and new units would replace those sold.[6]

Similar testimony was presented by Ira S. Robbins, president of the National Association of Housing and Redevelopment Officials (NAHRO). Based on the NAHRO Study of Low-Income Housing, recommendations for "provision for the sale of public housing units to tenants, under appropriate circumstances" were included in the Congressional hearings.[7]

While the advocates of cooperative tenure in public housing were forceful in presenting their recommendations, little documentation was offered that illustrated which social effects would occur if public rental projects were, in fact, converted to cooperative ownership. Aside from some economic benefits that would have accrued to both tenants and the public housing agency, the references to the social benefits of cooperatives remained hypothetical and unproven. One thing is certain--public housing policy had gathered many more critics and opponents than supporters, and it is a rare piece of housing literature that does not contain many reasons to castigate the program. It is well known that any recommendations for further change in national public housing tenure policy must be based on known deficiencies in the existing program. This point cannot be debated. Yet, these deficiencies must be viewed rationally and scientifically as to causal factors. This is especially true for changes in tenure policy, in that there have been no specific investigations of the relationship of the existing rental policy on

residents of public housing. Roger Starr alludes to
this research shortcoming in his challenge to the
critics of public housing--whose writings have contributed to the unpopularity of the program by Con-
gress--by noting how tragic it is that, perhaps, a
large portion of these critics have never entered
public housing development "or bothered to search
out the successful ones, or analyzed the qualities
of architecture, site selection, management, and size
that have made some more successful than others."[8]

To summarize this brief review of tenure policy
in public housing, it would be an understatement to
assert that public housing has never been a program
to catch people's imagination or to inspire great
civic pride. Its accomplishments have been overshadowed by its shortcomings, and policy makers are
reviewing the entire conceptual basis of the program
in view of these criticisms. In the last fifteen
years, the shift of emphasis at the national level
has been from programs aimed solely at the provision
of decent, safe and sanitary housing to programs
emphasizing total community development. In the
time since the Housing Act of 1937, which authorized
the present public housing program, national social
goals have changed substantially, particularly in
the past decade. Yet, the tenure policy of the public
housing program has remained virtually unchanged, in
spite of those who argue for experimentation. The
model for such experimentation has been well outlined
in what might be termed "the conceptual principles of
cooperative housing," as well as in the legislation
making this form of tenure possible.

PRINCIPLES OF COOPERATIVE HOUSING

In attempting to define "cooperative housing,"
one is immediately made aware of the semantic and
operational confusion that is associated with this
form of housing, particularly when it is compared to
"home ownership." Cooperative housing is supported
by a long history of cooperatives in other fields,
including retail cooperatives, agricultural cooperatives, consumer cooperatives, insurance cooperatives

and electric and telephone cooperatives. Like other forms of cooperatives, a housing cooperative is owned and controlled by the members and the cooperative association, or corporation, with each cooperator holding a share, or membership certificate, in the total stock of the housing corporation.

All too often, it is thought that the cooperative resident owns his apartment unit outright, when, in fact, he is actually part-owner of the entire development.[9] Jerome Liblit clarifies the operational definition of cooperative ownership by explaining that

> cooperative housing is a 'form' of home ownership in which the resident and his neighbors own their property jointly. It differs from public housing in that the overall policies of the project are controlled and determined by its members.[10]

For the most part, the literature on the subject fails to clearly define the operational, financial, legal and economic components of the term "ownership," as it is applied to cooperative housing. Promotional material made available by nationally famous cooperative organizations repeatedly refers to the number of families that achieved "home ownership" through the acquisition of cooperative apartments. Also present in such literature is a description of the full range of values and benefits purported to be derived from "home ownership" through cooperative housing.

The generic meaning of the term "ownership" in cooperative housing is a complexity of privileges, responsibilities and benefits inherent in the legal, administrative and financial elements of this form of tenure. The corporate nature of cooperative housing is difficult for most laymen to comprehend, so the specifics and details are conveniently grouped together under the parasol of "home ownership." This point is important to consider in this study, for the social effects presumed to be associated with cooperative tenure have been much influenced by the assumptions associated with the social effects of single-family home ownership. This comparison will become

apparent throughout this review. In most American
cooperatives, neither the individual apartment unit,
building nor grouping of buildings in a cooperative
housing development is owned by the residents per se.
Rather, a single cooperative housing corporation is
organized, which owns and operates, on a nonprofit
basis, the entire housing development for the benefit
of all its members. The cooperative housing corporation has title to the property and undertakes responsibility for the mortgage debt. Therefore, the housing
cooperative is mutually owned and controlled by its
residents, in that all the stock in the housing
corporation belongs to the tenant-cooperators. The
share, or membership certificate, held by a tenant-
owner entitles him to an occupancy agreement or the
equivalent of a lease on an individual apartment.
Although this share-owning form of housing cooperative
is most common, there are variations, which are discussed later.

As emphasized in the literature, the share
entitles the cooperator to an equal voting voice with
all other residents regarding the operation of the
housing development. What is referred to as "home
ownership" in the literature is, in actuality, ownership of a share in a housing corporation. This
technicality is poorly understood by most cooperative
housing residents, and they often are vague as to
their exact legal status as members of a housing
cooperative.

In general, the assumptions concerning the social
effects of cooperative housing center around the
beliefs that cooperative ownership is related to
active involvement in neighborly activities, to
participation in neighborhood functions and to the
willingness of individuals to work together toward
common goals and objectives. Concurrent with these
factors are the assumptions that

> cooperative home ownership at its best engen-
> ders pride in one's neighborhood. The spirit
> of mutual helpfulness in providing good homes
> and environment appears to create a group
> morale and group standards of conduct whose
> social value is hard to measure.[11]

This reference seems to affirm the fact that the
literature is void of quantifiable measures of the
social values mentioned. Jerry Voorhis broadens this
shortcoming, somewhat, in stating that the values
and benefits of cooperation result in "neighborhood
development and in the obtaining of needed supplies,
services and recreational facilities,"[12] thus postu-
lating that this form of tenure is conducive to
participation in activities oriented toward neighborhood improvement by tenant-cooperators.

Insofar as community participation and social
interaction are concerned, a policy statement of the
Cooperative League of the U.S.A. has asserted that
"housing co-ops have succeeded in bringing back the
spirit of neighborliness that had all but disappeared
from many low- and middle-income areas of our big
cities. They create feelings of permanence and sociability."[13] The same policy statement goes on to
state that "a co-op is a miniature democracy,"[14]
reinforcing the belief that cooperative housing
provides a setting for the training of residents in
the democratic process and is conducive to active
participation in decision-making that affects both
the cooperative and the larger community. These
statements presume that the cooperative principle
of democratic participation may function in all
human interaction. In promulgating the concept of
"one person, one vote," the ideal of equality, supposedly, becomes reality in cooperative housing. It
is argued that democracy in a cooperative means
that control is distributed to every member. Participation is supposed to be meaningful because the
assumption of responsibility by each member of the
cooperative is continually sought.

Underlying the theoretical premises concerning
cooperative tenure is the mutuality principle of
cooperative housing. Emory S. Bogardus defines this
term in explaining that "by mutuality is meant the
working together of self-respecting persons for the
good of all persons. In cooperating for the good of
all, perhaps we indirectly enrich their own lives
too."[15] The difficulty associated with measuring
the operational reality of this principle is complex
and challenging. The basic test of the principle of

mutuality is that cooperative residents recognize
the fact that they, actually, are part of a group,
organized according to a set of interrelated principles and norms and oriented toward operational goals
formulated from these principles and norms. The
problem of analysis becomes, largely, one of measuring
the extent to which residents do, in fact, perceive
their role in a cooperatively owned housing development and the degree to which they perceive their
fellow residents as being aware and willing to work
toward the goals established for the cooperative.
This theoretical concept is better defined as perception of community solidarity, as opposed to the
somewhat nebulous concept of "mutuality." The evaluation of solidarity by cooperative residents provides
a more realistic measure of the social effects of the
concept. The measure of community solidarity is
explained operationally in a later section of this
study.

In describing the dimensions of solidarity in
a cooperative housing development, it has been noted
that cooperative ownership, with its relative permanence, imposes upon residents of co-ops the need to
assume a positive attitude toward their neighbors,
an attitude based on feelings of community spirit
and mutual responsibility toward one another. Harold
N. Vogel states that, furthermore, cooperative ownership develops a willingness on the part of its residents to accommodate themselves to their fellow
residents "more than in a rented apartment or a
private house."[16] Furthermore, the group solidarity
supposedly developed through cooperative housing
engenders feelings of pride and responsibility toward
one's home. The belief that cooperative owners
develop a strong sense of responsibility toward the
maintenance of their development is one of the most
potent factors attributed to this form of tenure.
This point is made with considerable force in a
summary of remarks made at the 1963 Workshop on
Cooperative Housing:

> Membership concern for the proper maintenance
> of a cooperative housing development is per-
> haps one of the factors that awakens tenants

to the realization that they are in a different type of development than ordinary
rental or government housing. As long as
the owner or the government paid the cost
of broken windows and other vandalism,
residents could look on with indifference.
But when they become members of a cooperative they soon learn that the cost of vandalism must be shared by all the members
in terms of a higher budget and probably
higher rent for each of them. This soon
results in better care of the property.[17]

Of the many arguments posed concerning the
benefits of cooperative tenure, the savings-in-main-
tenance argument is most often heard. And like
many of the arguments concerning cooperative housing,
a polarization of opinion exists. On the positive
end of the scale, as asserted by Bogardus and others,
cooperative owners are believed to have greater pride
in their apartments and development and, therefore,
will personally involve themselves to see that both
their apartments and buildings are well maintained.
Challenging this belief, it has been argued that the
same motive for preserving property is present in
the case of those who rent apartments. Charles M.
Haar argues that "children of owner-members are more
apt to regard themselves as tenants in the face of
a centralized management,"[18] challenging the argument
that property damage is reduced by parents carefully
instructing their children to respect cooperatively
owned property.

To sum up the review of the basic assumptions
relating to cooperative housing, the following social
effects have been attributed to cooperative tenure:

1. Cooperatives are a community in themselves
and, yet, are part of a larger community.

2. Pride in the appearance of the cooperative,
as well as "keeping up" the cooperatively owned
property, is characteristic of cooperative ownership.

3. The spirit of mutual helpfulness that is

developed helps to create a group morale and mutual standards of conduct and group responsibility.

4. Cooperatives encourage working together to control neighborhood environment.

5. Cooperatives bring back the spirit of neighborliness and create feelings of permanence and sociability.

6. The social interaction of varied background groups is basic to a cooperative and is fostered by cooperative living.

7. Cooperative housing develops leadership potential through active participation in community activities.

8. Decisions are made on the subordination of individual considerations, so that decisions are made on the basis of what is best for the cooperative.

Before completing this examination, it is necessary to review some less emphatic opinions regarding those social effects listed above. In a preliminary investigation of cooperative housing developments conducted by the Office of Church and Housing of the United Presbyterian Church, the findings indicate that the traditional social justifications for cooperative housing are not entirely valid. The study showed that

it does not appear that cooperative living makes people more active in community organizations than they would have been anyway. Apparently most residents of cooperative housing are attracted more by the economic fact that it is good living at a low price than by the chance to be part of a community. Many consider themselves 'tenants' rather than 'cooperators,' insist their 'carrying charges' are no different from 'rent' and say that they simply do not feel that they are 'part landlords' as the cooperative movement insists. In other words, the fact that a cooperator is actually part of the

management does not lessen the traditional
landlord-tenant antagonism (unless he happens
to be one of the activists who is elected
to the Board).[19]

However, the article goes on to state:

> There is considerable evidence, however,
> that people who buy into a co-op primarily
> from economic motives will accept the idea
> that they will form friendships and social-
> ize within this group. A distinct contrast
> to most rental housing developments of the
> same economic level. . . . The fact that
> people are told they are cooperators seems
> to make them more open to possibilities of
> meeting with their neighbors than in similar
> rental housing.[20]

These statements are based on perfunctory investigations conducted in cooperative housing developments
in the Bronx, Queens and the Lower East Side. It
was shown in this overview of cooperatives in New
York City that participation by cooperative residents
in activities directed toward neighborhood improvement was not what the proponents of cooperative
housing claimed it would be. Grace Ann Goodman notes:

> It does not seem to be true that co-op resi-
> dents are motivated to work for general
> neighborhood improvement. . . . Co-op resi-
> dents tend to form themselves into an enclave
> to shut out the slums around. It is possible
> that the fact that they are cooperators may
> even intensify this tendency by predisposing
> them to cooperate with each other within the
> co-op development rather than joining exist-
> ing neighborhood social, educational, and
> recreational facilities.[21]

The rapidly increasing popularity that cooperative
housing is receiving is bound to produce healthy
debate as to the differences between cooperative and
rental tenure. Unfortunately, this debate is just
beginning to accelerate, and policy decisions have

already been made relying solely on hypotheses that
have not only been untested but remain, for the most
part, unchallenged. The development of a constructive
body of knowledge in an area of housing policy and
theory that is presently devoid of empirical research
is the goal toward which this study aims.

To a large extent, the testing of theoretical
assumptions and concepts depends on two important
factors related to cooperative housing--the education
of tenant-owners in the theory and principles of
cooperative housing and the type of sponsor that
develops the project initially. A brief review of
these two factors is necessary to place the material
reviewed in a more complete perspective. In that
the principles of cooperative housing are abstract
and highly idealistic, it is important to review
the means used to transmit theoretical concepts into
operational reality.

TENANT EDUCATION PROGRAMS

In many ways, the social effects of any housing
program are largely dependent on educating residents
to the general norms and values of the residential
development. Unheard of in most privately sponsored
multiple-dwelling projects, tenant education is a
basic component of cooperative housing and, to a
lesser extent, of public housing. Tenant education
is divided into pre-occupancy and post-occupancy stages.
Pre-occupancy cooperative education is essentially
designed to attract people to the idea of cooperative
housing, while post-occupancy education has one major
goal, which is "to convert a mass of relatively unknown
individuals who come together for one basic purpose
into a cohesive group which will function collectively
and constructively for the maximum and optimum development of this mutual effort."[22] The success or failure
of tenant education may affect the overall social
climate of a cooperative--by affecting the extent
that residents are both able and willing to understand
and accept the principles of cooperative housing.
"Basic to any education program is the ability to
inspire people, and to offer them some kind of

organization in which they will find a sense of
identity, a sense of belonging, a sense of participation."[23]

In addition to creating a socially cohesive
community, cooperative education aims toward influencing residents to participate in community-oriented
affairs. It has been stated that a functional goal
of cooperative housing is not only to solidify the
residents of the cooperative but to relate the
residents to the broader community in which they
live and to the role that they can play in the
community.[24] This far-reaching goal was incorporated
into the education program developed at Franklin
Plaza. The aims of the education program were twofold:
"to develop organic relationships in a community
situation which Franklin Plaza affords its tenant
owners," and "to prepare the residents for the intra-
and inter-community relations that come with living
with neighbors in a community."[25]

Communication with residents through on-going
education programs is an important aspect of cooperative housing and should, in turn, be an important
social force. It is presumed in this study that
transmission of the goals, values and philosophy of
cooperative housing is, to a large extent, dependent
on the education program devised and, more important,
on the degree to which cooperative residents are able
and willing to incorporate these concepts into their
everyday life. In that an active program of tenant
education was in existence at Franklin Plaza in the
form of newspapers and group forums, it will be both
interesting and meaningful to analyze the effects of
this program, as they are expressed in the hypotheses
being tested in this study.

Before completing this review with a summary of
the legislation and programs that encourage cooperative
housing, it is important to briefly review the various
types of cooperatives developed in this country.

VARIOUS APPROACHES TO COOPERATIVE HOUSING

It has been stated that there are two schools

of thought among current developers of cooperative
housing; one school of thought merely promotes
moderately priced housing, the other promotes "the
cooperative way of life," stressing the benefits of
cooperative organization.[26] The variance in goals
is most often dependent upon the source of sponsorship
for cooperative housing. Discounting luxury cooperatives, there are four types of sponsors responsible
for the majority of the moderately priced cooperatives
in the country.

Consumer Sponsor

This is, usually, a nonprofit group, such as a
trade union, a church or civic group or a settlement
house, which completely plans, and even builds, the
cooperatives before the memberships are assembled.
Usually, the consumer sponsor will contract with a
management group, such as the United Housing Foundation, the Foundation for Cooperative Housing or the
Association for Middle Income Housing, to supervise
the legal details, the financial arrangements, the
actual construction and the eventual renting and
management of the cooperative. This organization
might be likened to the cooperative housing building
societies found in Scandinavia and the Netherlands.
These organizations are prepared to deal with the
administrative and legal problems that groups and
developer-builders find themselves unprepared or
unwilling to deal with. The Federal Housing Administration (FHA) has adopted procedures that provide for
such arrangements, as has the State of New York.

The consumer-sponsored approach seems to eliminate
most risks for the eventual cooperative buyer, in that
most of the technical problems have already been
solved.[27] A further benefit of consumer-sponsored
cooperatives is that no member ever has to risk his
investment in a cooperative that may fail to take
title to the property.

Membership Sponsor

This is an existing membership group that

undertakes the process of building a cooperative housing development for its own use. It may also consist of a group of families who pool their resources together and carry out the entire process themselves. They must be willing to wait until plans are formulated, financial arrangements are made and construction is completed. Although the membership-sponsored approach comes closest to the theoretical or ideal meaning of cooperative housing, this type of cooperative is the most difficult to develop. There are many financial and administrative technicalities, which few amateur groups are able to master. In fact, Starr makes the point that "for every group that has formed spontaneously and successfully developed its own community for its members, a hundred have perished by the wayside."[28]

Builder Sponsor

As a result of mortgage financing for cooperatives made available under Section 213 of the 1949 National Housing Act, many private builders have entered the cooperative housing market. Private builders have also taken advantage of financing made available for cooperative housing in New York City and New York State under the provisions of the Private Housing Finance Law.[29] Few of the cooperatives built under this type of sponsorship were directed toward the lower-middle-income market and criticisms of the builders' lack of communication with future cooperators are common to this type of cooperative.[30]

Investor Sponsor

Less common is the investor-sponsored cooperative, in which a builder will sell a building, developed as a rental project, to a cooperative corporation. This type of sponsorship works best when a sponsor oversees the process and guarantees the builder that he will purchase the site when completed. In many ways, this approach resembles the "turnkey" approach currently popular in public housing.

In summation, it would appear that consumer-sponsored cooperatives most actively encourage the application of cooperative principles of living. Every effort is taken to acquaint prospective residents with the theoretical concept mentioned. The uniqueness of cooperative housing, both in terms of its financial and social benefits, is emphasized in marketing programs and is later incorporated into tenant education programs. Unlike builder-sponsored cooperatives, where the economic aspects are stressed solely, consumer sponsors appear to be cognizant of the social effects attributed to this form of tenure, and every effort is taken to convey these to residents.

The social effects claimed to be related to cooperative ownership have greatly affected public policy makers concerned with moderately priced housing and the more difficult task of community development. As already mentioned, a sizable body of literature has developed on the negative aspects of the public housing programs, which has influenced the direction taken in current housing policy. To complete this background review, a history of cooperative housing policy and the influence that many of the concepts and assumptions reviewed so far have had on those responsible for housing policy formulation are presented as a means of introducing this study.

HISTORY OF COOPERATIVE HOUSING
POLICY IN THE UNITED STATES

Experiments in the establishment of cooperative associations have been numerous, particularly in rural America. With regard to cooperative housing for low- and moderate-income urban families, only in recent years have the experiments assumed any meaningful proportion, although this proportion is still overshadowed by housing programs oriented toward single-family home ownership and the construction of rental apartments. To evaluate the social effects of cooperative housing, it is important to understand not only the theoretical premises and assumptions underlying the subject but, also, the legislation that has developed over the course of the past four decades.

By reviewing housing legislation relevant to tenure
policy, it becomes possible to extrapolate the
theoretical assumptions that have influenced the
legislation and the programs that have evolved.

The goal of home ownership has long been dominant
in the American value system. Home ownership was
articulated as a national value as early as 1932, when
President Hoover stated that "to possess one's own
home is the hope and ambition of almost every individual in our country. . . . That our people should live
in their own homes is a sentiment deep in the heart
of our race and American life."[31]

The sentiment toward home ownership has virtually
dominated national housing policy since the early
thirties and is, in many ways, synonymous with the
sentiments expressed regarding cooperative ownership.
However, the translation of the goal of home ownership
has not been sufficiently transmitted to the lower-
income segment of the population to any major extent.
New York State was the only state that recognized the
value of ownership and foresaw the need for not only
single-family home ownership but also cooperative
ownership of apartments, particularly for lower-middle-
income families.

The earliest legislation supporting cooperative
housing for this segment of the population was drawn
up six years before President Hoover's statement on
national housing policy was made. The New York State
Limited Dividend Corporation Act of 1926, often referred
to as the "Housing Companies Law," provided long-term
financing for a large number of cooperative units in
New York City. Some of the best-known cooperatives
in America were developed under this legislation.
Among these cooperatives were the Amalgamated Clothing
Workers of America cooperatives in the Bronx and in
the Lower East Side, which were built in 1927. This
act was a pioneering piece of legislation and was
formulated on the then popular conception that cooperatives were to be formed by a group of people working
together to finance and build their own housing. The
legislation was written "contemplating development by
groups of individuals banding together to build, or

have constructed for themselves, their housing."[32]
This idealized notion of cooperatives has its origin
in Scandinavia's efforts in cooperatively built and
owned housing, and the image alluded to prevails to
some extent today.

With the coming of the New Deal, government
intervention in housing grew in importance and became
part of the long-range recovery program. Housing was
considered mainly in economic and physical terms, and
programs were designed primarily to stimulate employment and business in the building industry. Improvement of social conditions was not a primary goal of
the housing program, nor was any effort made to support
cooperative ownership as one means of realizing
Hoover's hope of home ownership for all Americans.
With the passage of the National Industrial Recovery
Act of 1933, the groundwork was laid for the beginning
of a housing program, which, subsequently, developed
into a national public housing program. The Act
specified that the housing program of the Public Works
Administration was to include "construction, recon-
struction, alteration, or repair under public regulation or control of low-cost housing and slum clearance
projects."[33] Although "low-cost" might have been
interpreted as providing tenure forms other than
rental tenure, it seemed to imply only the latter.

The Housing Act of 1937 authorized the United
States Housing Authority to provide loans and annual
contributions to local public housing agencies for
low-rent housing and slum clearance projects. This
program of assistance is still the basis of the public
housing program now supervised by the Housing Assistance Administration of the Department of Housing
and Urban Development. The Housing Act of 1937 stipu-
lated many items that have a direct relation to the
discussion of tenure policies. The units to be provided were for rent only, and the rents of public
housing units were to be 20 percent below existing
rents in private rental housing. These provisions
not only specified rental tenure, but made it difficult
to alter the tenure policy without changing many of
the basic policies for the entire program.

The Federal Housing Act of 1949 was the first
national effort made to encourage the development of
moderate-priced cooperatives. Title I of the Act
authorized municipalities to acquire substandard
areas through the power of eminent domain and to sell
them below cost for redevelopment by private investors
and public agencies for predominantly residential
uses. In New York City, the Title I program was
utilized to develop the Morningside Gardens cooperative
and the International Ladies Garment Workers Union
(ILGWU) Village cooperative.[34] The Act was somewhat
revised in 1950, with the addition of Section 213,
which authorized the FHA to insure mortgages in
cooperative developments. Section 213 was the principal source of cooperative housing in the nation and,
especially in New York City, where, by the early
sixties, over 24,000 units were completed under this
FHA program. This regulation was an important program
for families with incomes higher than the maximum
set for other programs. Few moderate-income families,
however, could afford the units developed under this
program.

The Housing Act of 1956 added another dimension
to the Section 213 cooperative housing program. Under
this improved program, an investor could undertake
the entire obligation of securing the land and building
the project. The investor would then agree to sell
the completed project to a cooperative corporation
at a guaranteed price. If it cost less, the cooperative would pay less, but if it cost more, the cooperative would pay only the guaranteed upset price. All
down payments collected from cooperative members are
placed in an escrow account. They are used only
when the project is completed and when the cooperative
takes title--after it has sold sufficient memberships.
If the cooperative purchase is not completed, all of
the deposits are returned to the members. Thus, the
entire risk of completion and sale is assumed by the
investor--not by the cooperative or its members.
The down payments in FHA-financed cooperatives are
low, since the FHA-insured mortgage is 97 percent of
the project cost. This means that the typical down
payment will be 3 percent, plus 1 percent of the
cooperative's working capital, with no extra closing

costs. Again, these benefits were selective and affected those who could afford cooperatives at the price level established.

The most important piece of legislation that focused directly on lower-middle-income families was developed in New York State in 1955. During that year, the state of New York passed the Limited-Profit Corporations Law, popularly known as the "Mitchell-Lama Act." Under the law, the state and its cities may make 90 percent loans, repayable over fifty years, with interest at the rate paid by the state or city when it sells its bonds to raise the funds. Tax concessions for a maximum period of thirty years were also incorporated into this act. A new statute was passed in 1959 to create a new corporation, the state Housing Finance Agency, whose purpose is to provide a fund for financing cnnstruction by limited profit housing companies. State mortgage funds were made available through the Housing Finance Agency or through direct state loans. In 1960, additional legislation was passed allowing for conversion of some public projects constructed by the New York City Housing Authority to cooperatives, under the city's limited-profit program. This amendment was used initially in eight developments, which made available 7,268 units of cooperatively owned housing. Each project converted was sponsored by a nonprofit public interest group, so as to insure availability of the housing at the lowest possible price. Franklin Plaza originated as a result of this legislation.

Since 1960, several programs have been established in New York State to help families qualify for limited-profit (Mitchell-Lama) cooperatives. The Home Owners Purchase Endorsement plan (HOPE), administered by the State Commissioner of Housing, provides low-cost, ten-year loans, covering all but $200 of the down payment in cooperatives. The HOPE plan is available to financially stable familes who are able to meet the monthly carrying charges and repay the loan. The New York State Legislature has also approved increasing the amount of mortgage loans for cooperatives to 95 percent, thereby reducing the down payments required for projects built under the limited-profit housing program in the future.

The Housing Act of 1961, through FHA Section 221(d)(3), has provided cooperative apartments for below-average-income families. This FHA program is based on special financing provided by the Federal National Mortgage Association at interest rates that equal the current national average of federal borrowing. The program is limited to those families with below-average income for their community who qualify as to credit standing, thus demonstrating their need as well as eligibility and ability to assume the responsibility of cooperative tenure. The 221(d)(3) program can also be used to purchase and rehabilitate existing housing for cooperative ownership. This legislation, coupled with the Mitchell-Lama program in New York State, paved the way for Section 236 of the 1968 Housing Act and the Turnkey III program designed for public housing. These programs, coupled with Section 235 of the same act, evolved largely from Senator Charles H. Percy's proposals on the subject of home ownership for the poor.[35]

The general arguments for home ownership in the form of both single family homes and cooperative apartments were presented in Senator Percy's Home-ownership Agreement Plan. In elaborating on the proposal for local nonprofit housing associations, which would be organized by local people to sponsor housing, Percy foresaw the participation of families from moderate income down to the public housing eligibility levels that show promise of ability and desire to improve their economic level. These families would be counseled in the practice, responsibility and advantages of home ownership. Recognizing the scarcity of single-family homes in urban areas at prices that low- and moderate-income families can afford, Percy recommends the following policy in urban slums:

1. The formation of cooperatives to buy multifamily buildings or entire blocks of buildings for cooperative ownership

2. The conversion of existing public housing buildings into owner-cooperatives

3. The provision of assistance for individuals to become owners of their public

> housing units in exercising lease-with-
> option-to-purchase options under exist-
> ing federal leased housing and rent
> subsidy programs.[36]

The arguments presented in favor of ownership
of this nature are, probably, the most powerfully
stated of any so far. It is suggested that the
force of conviction with which they are presented
had a great deal to do with influencing the home
ownership proposal for the 1968 Housing and Urban
Development Act. Although not as yet documented, it
can safely be said that a major step in refocusing
national housing policy for the urban slum has been
taken on the basis of relatively vague and idealistic
assumptions that prevail in the literature, not only
for cooperative housing but for the general program
of home ownership. In that this study is aimed at
policy-making as well as theory-building, it is im-
perative that Percy's arguments advocating ownership
and the conversion of public rental projects into
cooperatively owned projects be related to this
research. In summary, the underlying basis of the
Percy plan as well as the proposals of others regarding
cooperative tenure rests on Percy's belief that

> of absolutely crucial importance to any such
> program is the central element of home owner-
> ship. For a man who owns his own home ac-
> quires a new dignity. He begins to take
> pride in what is his own, and pride in con-
> serving and improving it for his children.
> He becomes a more steadfast and concerned
> citizen of his community. He becomes self-
> confident and self-reliant. Becoming a
> homeowner transforms him. It gives him roots,
> a sense of belonging, a true stake in the
> community and its well-being.[37]

In reviewing the development of national and
state legislation on cooperative ownership of housing,
the underlying belief in the positive effects of ownership becomes apparent. While this study is not oriented
toward the positive and negative values of home ownership as a goal for American housing policy, the point

must be raised, insofar as the legislation and ensuing
policy decisions are greatly influenced by the assumed
effects on the social well-being of home owners.
Needless to add, the proponents of cooperative housing
as a substitute for single-family home ownership,
particularly in slum neighborhoods, have incorporated
both the facts and myths concerning the social effects
of ownership. In undertaking this study, a statement
made by John P. Dean provided a useful delineation
between the real and the imagined effects of cooperative housing and bears repeating in light of the
above review of legislative decisions resting on
unresearched assumptions: "As a value built deeply
into the culture, the pro-ownership sentiment has
remained relatively free from attack, and little need
has been felt to justify it."[38] The question to be
answered is whether proposals regarding the conversion
of public housing projects into cooperatives can be
justified on the actuality of the social effects
presumed related to cooperative ownership.

SUMMARY

In reviewing the major themes that have developed
regarding cooperative tenure and its social effects,
the belief that cooperative ownership of housing does
influence social behavior has been widely accepted
and remains virtually unchallenged. Even though there
have been no major studies that have examined the
social effects of this form of tenure in relation to
rental tenure, major policy decisions have emerged,
based, largely, on assumptions and instinct.

Without a body of research from which to examine
and formulate hypotheses, the formulation of hypotheses
to test in this study has had to emanate from descriptive literature rather than from a literature that is
empirically based. The structural framework of this
study, then, is oriented toward the provision of
empirically based answers to what might be termed
normative assumptions of relationships. The behavioral
and descriptive data gathered for this study should
establish a framework from which to analyze this range
of assumptions.

It remains unproven that cooperative tenure is, in part, related to the social effects attributed to it when control variables are used in an analysis of relationships. Does cooperative housing provide a conducive setting for neighborly interaction, or is it really no different than a similar rental project? Is the desire to be part of a cooperative more important than the need for reasonably priced housing? Is cooperative ownership perceived to be like home ownership? Are the residents of cooperative housing projects functionally integrated into the larger community and willing to work for its betterment, or do they merely isolate themselves from it? The number of unanswered questions is formidable, and their answers are vital to contemporary housing policy. It is hoped, therefore, that the findings of this study will provide a constructive body of knowledge concerning an aspect of housing policy and theory that is in need of empirical research.

NOTES

1. Of all the critical literature on the program, the most realistic approach to the problems associated with public housing is found in Catherine Bauer Wurster, "The Dreary Deadlock of Public Housing," in William L. C. Wheaton et al., eds., Urban Housing (New York: The Free Press, 1966), pp. 245-51.

2. Wurster, "Social Questions in Housing and Community Planning," Journal of Social Issues, VII, Nos. 1 and 2 (1951), 1-33.

3. Glenn H. Beyer, Housing: A Factual Analysis (New York: The Macmillan Company, 1958), p. 250.

4. Robert M. Fisher, Twenty Years of Public Housing (New York: Harper and Brothers, 1939), p. 245.

5. Ernest M. Fisher, "A Study of Housing Programs and Policies" (Washington, D.C.: Housing and Home Finance Agency, 1960), p. 297.

6. Hearings on H.R. 5840 and Related Bills,

U.S. House of Representatives, Subcommittee on Housing
of the Committee on Banking and Currency (89th Cong.,
1st sess.) (Washington, D.C.: Government Printing
Office, 1965), Part I, p. 323.

    7. Ibid., p. 439.

    8. Roger Starr, The Living End: The City and
Its Critics (New York: Coward-McCann, Inc., 1966),
p. 92.

    9. Lewis M. Isaacs, Jr., "'To Buy or Not to
Buy: That is the Question' . . . What's a Cooperative Apartment?," The Record (Association of the Bar
of the City of New York), XIII, No. 4 (April, 1958),
207.

    10. Jerome Liblit, ed., Housing--The Cooperative
Way (New York: Twayne Publishers, Inc., 1964), p. 71.

    11. Jerry Voorhis, American Cooperatives (New York:
Harper Brothers, 1961), p. 46.

    12. Ibid., p. 50.

    13. Cooperative League of the U.S.A., "Plus Values
in Cooperative Housing" (Chicago: Cooperative League
of the U.S.A., 1962), p. 5.

    14. Ibid., p. 5.

    15. Emory S. Bogardus, "Principles of Cooperation"
(Chicago: Cooperative League of the U.S.A., 1958),
Part II.

    16. Harold N. Vogel, The Co-op Apartment (New
York: Libra Publishers, Inc., 1960), p. 2.

    17. Workshop on Cooperative Housing (September,
1963), FCH Company, "Managing a Housing Co-op: Financial Aspects", in Liblit, ed., op. cit., pp. 152-53.

    18. Charles M. Haar, "Middle-Income Housing:
The Cooperative Snare?," Land Economics, XXIX (November,
1953), 289-94.

19. Grace Ann Goodman, "Cooperative Housing for Middle-Income Families in the New York City Area," in Mission Through Housing (New York: Office of Church and Housing, United Presbyterian Church in the U.S.A., 1967), p. 49.

20. Ibid., p. 50.

21. Ibid., p. 50.

22. Clara Fox, "Pre-Occupancy and Post-Occupancy Education," in Jerome Liblit, ed., op. cit., p. 157.

23. Ibid., p. 157.

24. Principles of Membership Education in Housing Cooperatives, Proceedings of a seminar sponsored by the New York State Division of Housing and Community Renewal, May 6, May 21 and June 4, 1964, (Albany: New York State Division of Housing and Community Renewal, 1964), pp. 1-10.

25. Letter to John Merli, President, Franklin Plaza Apartments, Inc., from S. F. Boden, Association for Middle-Income Housing, April 19, 1962.

26. Goodman, op. cit., p. 50.

27. Foundation for Cooperative Housing, "Cooperative Development with Federal Assistance--The Foundation for Cooperative Housing," in Liblit, ed., op. cit., p. 227.

28. Starr, "How cooperatives Are Formed," in Liblit, ed., op. cit., p.188.

29. Ibid., p. 190.

30. For the advantages of the builder-sponsored cooperative, see Martin Meyerson et al., Housing, People, and Cities (New York: McGraw-Hill Book Company, Inc., 1962), p. 213.

31. President's Conference on Home Building and Home Ownership, Housing and The Community--Home Repair

and Remodelling (Washington, D.C.: Government Printing
Office, 1932) Vol. IV, p. 30.

32. S. F. Boden, "Has Cooperative Housing Come
of Age? . . . The Association for Middle-Income
Housing," in Liblit, ed., op. cit., p. 215.

33. Robert K. Brown, The Development of the
Public Housing Program in the United States (Atlanta:
Georgia State College of Business Administration,
1960), p. 6.

34. Citizens' Housing and Planning Council of
New York, Inc., Directory of Large Scale Rental and
Cooperative Housing (New York: Citizens' Housing
and Planning Council of New York, 1957), p. 10.

35. Charles H. Percy, "A New Dawn for our Cities--
The Homeownership Achievement Plan," in Federal Role
in Urban Affairs, Senate Committee on Government
Operations, (Washington, D.C.: Government Printing
Office, 1966), Part 7, pp. 1437-45.

36. Ibid., pp. 1440-41.

37. Ibid., p. 1143.

38. John P. Dean, Home Ownership: Is It Sound?
(New York: Harper and Brothers, 1945), p. 2.

3

This study is viewed as a means of providing empirical data on the social and economic character- istics of residents of a variety of housing environ- ments in an urban low-income community. In that the study analyzes the social characteristics of low- and moderate-income families in East Harlem housing developments the data collected for this study are relevant to future research efforts, not only in the field of housing but also in those areas of study related to community organization and family life in below-average-income communities.

PROFILE OF THE STUDY AREA

The area serving as the locale for this study is the East Harlem community of New York City, where the three housing developments being examined are located. The boundaries of East Harlem are well delineated, bounded, on the east, by the East River and, on the north, by the Harlem River. The western boundary runs along Central Park, or Fifth Avenue, until East 119th Street, where the elevated tracks of the New York Central Railroad along Park Avenue serve as a physical boundary between East Harlem and Central Harlem. The southern boundary is the most striking of all, in that it is at East 96th Street that East Harlem ends and the Upper East Side of New York begins. It is at 96th Street that the railroad tracks are submerged under Park Avenue, and expensive apartment buildings and town houses replace the tenements and projects found to the north of this street.

DEMOGRAPHIC CHARACTERISTICS

The preponderance of nonwhites and Puerto Ricans is a significant characteristic of the population of East Harlem. Although the total population decreased by 22 percent in the decade from 1950 to 1960, the percentage of nonwhites and Puerto Ricans increased significantly, replacing a large Italian population. In 1960, whites constituted 24 percent of the population in East Harlem. Nonwhites constituted 29 percent in East Harlem, while Puerto Ricans constituted 46 percent of the total population, by far the largest sector of the population (see Table 1). Projected estimates for 1970 show a continuation of these trends, with nonwhites increasing in their relative proportion of the East Harlem population.

TABLE 1

Population, by Racial and Ethnic Group,
In East Harlem, Compared with Manhattan and New York City, 1960

Racial and Ethnic Group	East Harlem Number	East Harlem Percent	Manhattan Percent	New York City Percent
White	35,229	24.4	61.6	77.4
Nonwhite	42,217	29.2	25.1	14.7
Puerto Rican	67,090	46.4	13.3	7.9
Total	144,536	100.0	100.0	100.0

Source: New York City Department of City Plan-
ning, Special United States Census
Tabulations, 1960 (New York: New York
City Department of City Planning 1963).

The median age of the population of East Harlem
is twenty-five years, ten years lower than the median
for New York City. Nonwhite residents had a median
age of twenty-two years in 1960, while Puerto Ricans
had a median age of twenty-one years. In contrast
the white residents' median age was thirty-eight
years, reflecting a large concentration of elderly
white residents in East Harlem (see Table 2).

TABLE 2

Age Distribution, by Racial and Ethnic
Group, in East Harlem, Compared
with Manhattan and New York
City, 1960

| Age | East Harlem Area | | Manhattan | New York City |
	Number	Percent	Percent	Percent
Total Population:				
19 and Under	62,228	43.1	24.8	30.2
20-59	68,577	47.4	56.6	53.9
60 and Over	13,728	9.5	18.6	15.9
Total	144,533	100.0	100.0	100.0
Median Age	(24.9)		(37.6)	(35.0)
White Population:				
19 and Under	9,949	28.3	17.8	27.2
20-59	17,373	49.4	57.4	54.0
60 and Over	7,839	22.3	24.8	18.8
Total	35,161	100.0	100.0	100.0
Median Age	(38.5)		(44.6)	(38.5)

TABLE 2 Cont'd

Age	East Harlem Area		Manhattan Percent	New York City Percent
	Number	Percent		
Nonwhite Population:				
19 and Under	19,925	47.1	31.3	36.7
20-59	19,689	46.6	58.2	55.5
60 and Over	2,658	6.3	10.5	7.8
Total	42,282	100.0	100.0	100.0
Median Age	(22.1)		(32.6)	(28.9)
Puerto Rican Population:				
19 and Under	32,344	48.2	45.2	46.3
20-59	31,515	47.0	50.5	50.1
60 and Over	3,231	4.8	4.2	3.5
Total	67,090	100.0	100.0	100.0
Median Age	(21.2)		(22.6)	(21.9)

Source: New York City Department of City Plan-
ning, Special United States Census
Tabulations, 1960 (New York: New York
City Department of City Planning, 1963).

Household size was larger in East Harlem than
the median household size for New York City. The
median number of persons in occupied housing units
in East Harlem was 3.2 persons, compared to 2.5
persons for the city. Twenty-six percent of the
households in East Harlem contained five or more
persons, compared to 15 percent for New York City.
This pattern does not hold true when tabulated against
ethnic and racial groups. The variations in East
Harlem ranged from the white median of 2.2 persons
to the nonwhite median of 3.2 and the Puerto Rican
median of 4.3 persons.

SOCIOECONOMIC CHARACTERISTICS

East Harlem is characterized by its concentration of poverty-level families. A large portion of the area is incorporated within the Harlem Model Cities Neighborhood, and the community is currently the focus of a multitude of antipoverty programs, including a controversial decentralized school district. The educational level of persons twenty-five years old and over in East Harlem in 1960 was markedly lower than that of New York City. Only 4 percent of East Harlem residents had received some college education, while 8.7 percent of the residents had no formal education. The majority of persons living in East Harlem, 57 percent, received only an elementary school education (see Table 3). Unfortunately, estimates of these data for 1970 show little change, in spite of massive efforts in the field of educational planning.

TABLE 3

Educational Level of Persons Twenty-five
Years Old and Older, in East Harlem,
Compared with Manhattan and
New York City, 1960

School Level Completed	East Harlem Area Number	East Harlem Area Percent	Manhattan Percent	New York City Percent
No School	6,278	8.7	4.3	5.1
Elementary (1-8)	41,311	57.3	36.7	37.5
High School (1-4)	21,725	30.2	36.7	42.1
College	2,880	4.1	22.3	15.3
Total	72,194	100.0	100.0	100.0

Source: New York City Department of City Planning, Special United States Census Tabulations, 1960 (New York: New York City Department of City Planning, 1963).

Characteristic of East Harlem is the large
proportion of low-income families. The median
income of about $3,650 in 1959 for East Harlem was
far lower than the median of $6,100 for New York
City. While income levels have increased, it is
more than likely that the disparity remains proportionately constant in 1971. In 1959, 71 percent of
East Harlem residents had yearly incomes of less
than $5,000, compared to 36 percent in New York City.
The differences in income were fewer than those that
existed for the rest of the city, reflecting the
fact that the white population was predominantly
elderly and living on fixed incomes (see Table 4).

TABLE 4

Median Family Income in 1959, by Racial
and Ethnic Groups, in East Harlem,
Compared with Manhattan and
New York City, 1960

Racial and Ethnic Group	East Harlem	Manhattan	New York City
All Families:	$3,658	$5,338	$6,091
White	4,612	6,640	6,600
Nonwhites	3,579	4,045	4,437
Puerto Rican	3,337	3,459	3,811

Source: New York City Department of City Plan-
ning, Special United States Census
Tabulations, 1960 (New York: New York
City Department of City Planning, 1963).

The high unemployment rate for East Harlem, 9
percent, is a further parameter of the low socioeconomic status of the residents of this community. In
spite of the accelerated growth in the national
economy, as well as in the city, the unemployment
rate of the total labor force in 1971 remains at

over twice the national unemployment average. As
would be expected, only 9 percent of white residents
and 5 percent of nonwhites in East Harlem that were
employed were classified as professionals or managers
(see Table 5).

TABLE 5

Occupation of the Employed, in East
Harlem, Compared with Manhattan
and New York City, 1960

| Occupation | East Harlem Area | | Manhattan | New York City |
	Number	Percent	Percent	Percent
Professional and Technical	2,050	4.5	14.9	11.1
Managers and Officials	1,416	3.1	9.9	8.7
Clerical	5,676	12.5	17.8	21.2
Sales	1,398	3.1	5.5	7.0
Craftsmen and Foremen	3,661	8.1	6.0	10.4
Operators, household and Service Workers	24,067	53.0	33.9	31.1
Laborers	2,867	6.3	3.0	3.3
Not Reported	4,293	9.5	9.0	7.1
Total	45,408	100.0	100.0	100.0

Source: New York City Department of City Plan-
ning, Special United States Census
Tabulations, 1960 (New York: New York
City Department of City Planning, 1963).

HOUSING CHARACTERISTICS

The structural conditions of housing in East
Harlem reflect the low socioeconomic complexion of
the area. Aside from government-sponsored housing,
34 percent of the units in East Harlem's housing
stock was deteriorating in 1960, while 10 percent of
the occupied housing units in East Harlem were dilap-
idated. The deterioration rate was 23 percent higher
than the rate for the city, while the dilapidation
rate was 7 percent higher.[1] The 1960 census data on
the quality of occupied housing units in East Harlem
indicates that 15 percent were substandard, compared
to 9 percent for the remainder of New York City.
Current estimates show some reduction in the percent
of substandard units, but of minor proportions.

PUBLIC HOUSING IN EAST HARLEM

East Harlem has a higher concentration of public
housing projects than any other neighborhood in New
York City. One out of three East Harlem residents
is a tenant of the public Housing Authority. The
statistics on the major projects in East Harlem
indicate that they are fairly stable. In her book
on East Harlem, Patricia Cayo Sexton states that

> overwhelmingly, project families are self-
> supporting. Only 14 percent are on public
> welfare, and only 23 percent are consid-
> ered "problem families." The projects
> give the transient slum neighborhood
> (East Harlem) both stability and conti-
> nuity. Turnover in the projects, in-
> cluding transfer to other projects, has
> been very low, about 5 percent a year.[2]

Like most public housing in New York City, the East
Harlem projects appear to be well managed, and the
waiting lists for apartments are long. However,
this positive note does not mean that public housing
in East Harlem has escaped criticism. Public housing
in this community has been both praised and criticized,

as it has been throughout the country. The bulldozer era of public housing did not escape East Harlem, and many sound and architecturally important old buildings were removed in order to assemble large tracts of land for housing projects. Poor housing design, overly stringent rules, inadequate relocation provisions and failure to consult community leaders were some of the criticisms directed toward East Harlem's public housing program. More important to the social health of the community was the failure to build economically integrated housing, a criticism that dominates American public housing policy. With the exception of Lexington Houses, all of the projects were built specifically for low-income families. Families who earned more than a set maximum income could not apply; families who moved in and whose income rose above that maximum were supposed to move out.

Yet, in spite of the criticisms, public housing in East Harlem has provided good housing accommodations in the midst of an urban slum. Sexton documents this appraisal by quoting a local resident's opinion of the program:

> The projects brought islands of hope to
> many people in our community, scores of
> new parks and playgrounds, and many commu-
> nity centers which provide our residents
> with the opportunity to experiment in
> civic leadership. Many tenant associations
> are forming, and a new spirit of concern
> and participation in community life is
> coming forth.[3]

It is in this low-income community that this study has been carried out. The extent to which this environment has influenced the findings of this study will become evident throughout the analysis of the data presented. It must be noted that in the period since Sexton published her findings, the proportion of welfare tenants has increased in the public housing projects of East Harlem.

LEXINGTON HOUSES

The Lexington Houses were built under a New York City-aided program, known as the City III program, in 1951. This municipally financed project is similar to forty-eight public-aided housing projects in New York City that were built specifically for moderate-income families. Through the New York State program for public housing, as well as New York City's own program, families with incomes ranging from $6,192 to $9,036 may find reasonably priced apartments in these projects.[4] Unlike low-income public projects in New York City, which are, for the most part, federally aided, little has been written on the social environment of this form of public housing.

Lexington Houses consist of four concrete tower buildings, each being fourteen stories high. The project is located seven blocks south of Franklin Plaza, on a 3.5-acre site, bounded by Third and Park Avenues, between East 98th and 99th Streets. There are 448 apartments, with one- and two-bedroom units. Carrying charges average $21.45 per room. There is a playground, landscaped grounds and a community center on the present site. The total population of the project is 1,295.

JEFFERSON HOUSES

The Jefferson Houses were built as a low-income housing project in 1959 through the federal public housing program. Jefferson Houses consist of eighteen residential buildings, ranging in height from seven to fourteen stories. The project is located four blocks north of Franklin Plaza, on a seventeen-acre site, bounded by Third and First Avenues, between East 112th and 115th Streets. There are 1,493 apartments in the project, with a total estimated population of 5,600. Monthly rents per room average $13.00. There is a community center, public school and a variety of recreational facilities on the site. Although the grounds and buildings do not appear to be as carefully maintained as Lexington Houses, this

can be partially explained by the fact that 52 percent
of the total population are under eighteen years of
age, while, at Lexington Houses, only 32 percent of
the population were under eighteen.[5]

FRANKLIN PLAZA COOPERATIVE

Franklin Plaza consists of fourteen reinforced-
concrete tower buildings, each being twenty stories
high. It is located in the geographic heart of East
Harlem, on a fourteen-acre site, bounded by Third
and First Avenues, between East 105th and 108th
Streets. There are 1,635 apartments, ranging from
one- to three-bedroom units. Carrying charges average
$22.84 per room, with an equity investment of $450
per room. The investment can be financed over a
five-year period under the HOPE Program (described
in Chapter 8). There are ten acres of landscaped
grounds, including play areas, fountain pools, shuf-
fleboard and basketball courts and an outdoor theater.
Two public schools are adjacent to the site, and a
nursery school is in operation for members of the
cooperative.

Franklin Plaza was originally scheduled to
become a moderate-income public housing project, to
be rented by the New York City Housing Authority.
The project was originally developed by the Authority
as Benjamin Franklin Houses, a municipally aided
public project, through the no-cash subsidy program.
Under the provisions of Article 12, Section 58, of
the Public Housing Law of New York, the Housing
Authority was authorized to sell the project to a
cooporation created pursuant to the Limited-Profit
Housing Companies Law (the so-called Mitchell-Lama
Law) on a cooperative basis. This transaction was
subject to the approval of the City Planning Commission and the Board of Estimate of the city of New
York.

A sponsoring committee of twelve East Harlem
clergymen, settlement house directors, merchants and
politicians each pledged $5,000 to furnish the seed
money to make the cooperative possible. Each of

these twelve leaders was actively involved in East
Harlem and was a strong force behind the original
decision to introduce cooperative housing to the
community. The Franklin Plaza Housing Company was
established, with the sponsors of the cooperative
serving as directors and officers of the housing
company until the transfer of title to the project
from the Housing Authority to the Housing Company
took place.

The conversion of the project to cooperative
housing was the result of the influence of East
Harlem leaders, as well as members of the Housing
Authority. Local leaders in the East Harlem were
against the building of additional public housing in
a community that already had more than its share of
low-income projects, even though Benjamin Franklin
Houses were planned as a moderate-income project.
The New York City Housing Authority was sympathetic
to this view and was anxious to experiment with its
program. At the 1960 Conference on Cooperative
Housing, Ira Robbins, a member of the Authority,
announced the conversion of eight public housing
projects into cooperatively owned developments and
explained the benefits that would result. The proceedings of this portion of the conference were
summarized by Jerry Voorhis as follows:

> Mr. Robbins stated that the New York City
> Authority had decided to build eight proj-
> ects with homes for more than seven thou-
> sand families, and instead of maintaining
> them as publicly-owned housing, to sell
> them as cooperatives to the families who
> would live in them. It was well known
> that serious social problems have been
> arising with so-called 'public-housing.'
> Perhaps some of these could be solved by
> a new and extended use of cooperative
> methods and cooperative ownership.[6]

The sale of apartments was made pursuant to the
Certificate of Incorporation and the By-Laws of the
Franklin Plaza Housing Company. Tenant-cooperators
were given occupancy of their selected apartments as

tenants of the Housing Company as soon as the transfer of title took place. The project was still under
construction in August, 1961, when the initial legal
and administrative requirements were worked out.
The transfer of title took place on March 8, 1965,
almost four years after the planning began. During
the interim period, the Occupancy Agreement required
that the tenant subscriber pay the monthly estimated
carrying charges as rent during the period between
his date of occupancy of the project and the date
of purchase of the property by the Housing Company
from the Authority.

The first building of the project was completed
and ready for occupancy and delivered to the Franklin
Plaza Housing Company under the above arrangements
in December, 1961. The remaining buildings were
turned over at intervals thereafter. The last building was turned over on November 30, 1962. From the
time of initial possession under the lease, the
project had been managed by the Association for
Middle Income Housing Management Services. The
Housing and Redevelopment Board of New York City
(since incorporated into the Housing and Development
Administration) and the New York City Housing Authority approved the management agreement and supervised
the officers of the Franklin Plaza Housing Company.
Since Franklin Plaza is a state-subsidized cooperative, receiving a municipal tax exemption, the Housing
and Development Administration acts as the official
public agency supervising rental policy and acting
as a clearinghouse for information for the cooperative.

Initially, the Housing and Redevelopment Board
estimated that it would require at least two full
years to achieve full occupancy.[7] The actual time
involved to sell the cooperative units proved the
two-year market judgment to be optimistic. The
marketing of Franklin Plaza was adversely affected
by a variety of factors. The location of moderate-
income housing in the midst of an area known primarily
for its low-rent public housing and typed as an urban
slum did not facilitate sales. However, this may
not have been a major factor had the goal of integration not been made a prerequisite of the renting
program.

In order to achieve maximum integration in a
project that would normally be predominantly occupied
by Negro and Puerto Rican residents, it was decided,
in September, 1963, to discourage Negroes from applying
for apartments in order to maintain the level of racial
integration that had been developed by this date.[8]
A referral program was instituted whereby Negro
applicants were asked to seek middle-income housing
at two other developments where white families predominated. Although no qualified Negro applicants
were turned down, efforts were made to "point out to
them that Negro and white residents believe that
integration can best be served if the current racial
balance at the co-op is preserved."[9] At the time
this policy was initiated, over 50 percent of the
co-op's residents were Negroes, and there was a
sizable Puerto Rican population. The program was
initiated by the Tenant Liaison Committee, representing
families then living at Franklin Plaza. The action
taken was debated for a period of three months, and
a biracial study committee had been involved in
studying the legal and moral principles involved.

Compounded with the difficulty of attracting
white families to East Harlem, there were problems
involved regarding the sale of the apartments as a
result of design factors. The major demand in East
Harlem was for large apartments to serve families
with several children and for one-bedroom apartments
for childless families, usually elderly couples, who
previously lived in the community. Out of a total
of 1,635 apartments at Franklin, 1,072 were two-
bedroom units. These apartments proved to be most
difficult to sell, and by January 1, 1963, only 61
percent of these units were sold, while all the one-
bedroom units had been sold, and 94 percent of the
three-bedroom apartments were sold. Although there
was demand for housing at Franklin Plaza, the
restricted choice in the type of apartments available
delayed the marketing of the development.

The fact that cooperative housing was unknown
in East Harlem, coupled with the fact that Franklin
Plaza was almost identical in the basic physical
design of its buildings to most of the low-income

public housing projects in the community, caused
some initial trepidation on the part of potential
residents. To encourage prospective tenant-owners
to buy what they otherwise would have leased, the
New York City Housing Authority found it necessary
to install a number of additional amenities, above
its usual pattern, at a cost of approximately $1
million. These included such "amenities" as locked
doors at each building entrance, a private intercom
to the lobby from each apartment and on-site shopping.
It is interesting to note that in the flyers used to
advertise the cooperative, these basic features are
referred to as "luxury items." It was also necessary
to redesign the site plan of the original public
housing rental project in order to attract potential
cooperative owners. Albert Mayer was hired as a
consultant to the New York City Housing Authority to
transform the typically sterile and boring public
housing site plan into landscaped gardens and a
recreation plaza for adults and children. Mayer's
design was so successful that it received nationwide
recognition and the "plaza" is a major focal point
for all of East Harlem. It is interesting to note
that similar site plans are now incorporated into
most public housing projects proposed for New York
City, and extensive work is being carried out to
redesign existing public areas in New York's housing
projects, including many in East Harlem.

Financing of the project was undertaken under a
mortgage from the city of New York, an equity loan
from the New York State Housing Finance Agency and
the paid-in equity of the tenant cooperators. On
March 8, 1965, Franklin Plaza Apartments, Inc.
(formerly, the Franklin Plaza Housing Company),
acquired title to the housing development. The
property was purchased from the New York City Housing
Authority at a price equal to the total development
costs incurred by the Housing Authority. The Franklin
Plaza Company had amassed a capitalization of
$3,305,000 at the time of title transfer, and a
total number of shares consisted of 330,500 shares,
each having a par value of $10. All of the shares
of the cooperative have been allocated to the apartments in the project. Ownership of the respective

blocks of stock designated for each apartment entitles
each purchaser to an Occupancy Agreement, which allows
the purchaser to occupy the space to which his stock
is allocated. Each block of stock is represented by
one certificate. Regardless of the dollar amount of
his investment and the number of shares owned, each
tenant-cooperator has one vote on corporate matters
concerning which stockholders are entitled to vote.

In addition, the equity investment provided by
the stock subscriptions, a permanent mortgage for
$28,595,000, was obtained by Franklin Plaza Apartments,
Inc., from the city of New York, in the form of a
fifty-year self-liquidating permanent mortgage loan,
at a rate of interest equal to the cost of interest
to the city. At the time of transfer, the corporation
paid interest at the rate of 3.7 percent, plus .5
percent per annum, to cover the city's expenses of
borrowing and of administration, making a total of
4.2 percent. In 1968, increased mortgage interest
rates resulted in an increase in the cost of operating
the project, necessitating a 15 percent raise in
monthly maintenance costs for all residents.

SUMMARY

In examining the social, economic and environmental characteristics of East Harlem, it is immediately apparent that the residents of Franklin Plaza
and the Lexington Houses share few of these characteristics, aside from a similarity of racial and ethnic
backgrounds. The residents of Jefferson Houses,
being low-income families, are more like their East
Harlem neighbors. The question must be posed as to
whether neighborhood environmental conditions, both
physical and social, have had a significant effect
on the variables being tested, particularly the
solidarity and community participation variables.
The possible effects might range from active involvement to improve the surrounding slum neighborhood to
complete isolation from East Harlem, its residents,
institutions and activities. In that current housing
policy advocates the development of heterogeneous
urban communities, the findings of this study will

provide valuable insights into the actual effects
that are associated with the infusion of moderate
income families into a lower-class community.

A related aspect of this question concerns the
extent to which the Franklin Plaza Cooperative has
stimulated the aspirations and motivations of residents of public housing toward the goal of cooperative
ownership. How significant has Franklin Plaza been
in providing an impetus for public housing residents
to work toward the realization of cooperative ownership? Do the tenants of public housing recognize
Franklin Plaza and cooperative ownership as being
more desirable than renting in public housing? An
even more important question concerns whether tenants
of public housing would encourage and support the
conversion of their projects into cooperatives if
such policy were to be initiated. These questions
and the answers to them are relevant not only to
this study but to contemporary housing policy directed
toward the urban slum and its residents.

The chapters that follow set out to test several
hypotheses, as well as to provide answers to the
series of policy-related questions mentioned in
Chapter 2 and in this chapter. Chapter 4 will present
a statistical profile of the relevant socioeconomic
and demographic characteristics of the sample population. Chapter 5 examines levels of neighborly interaction, while Chapter 6 examines the concept of
community solidarity. Participation in the East
Harlem community is analyzed in Chapter 7, and Chapter
8 covers general housing attitudes. The concluding
chapter, 9, will provide a synthesis of the findings
of this study and recommendations for future housing
policy and research efforts.

NOTES

1. Housing and Redevelopment Board, "Social
and Economic Analysis of the East River Urban Renewal
Area" (New York: Housing and Redevelopment Board,
March, 1965), pp. 12-13.

2. Patricia Cayo Sexton, Spanish Harlem (New
York: Harper & Row, 1965), pp. 36-37.

3. Ibid., p. 39.

4. New York City Housing Authority, "1967
Guide to Housing Developments," (New York: New York
City Housing Authority, 1967), p. 4.

5. New York City Housing Authority, Statistics
Division, "Project Data: Characteristics of Tenants
as of January 1, 1967" (New York: 1967).

6. Jerry Voorhis, American Cooperatives (New
York: Harper Brothers, 1961), pp. 51-52.

7. Housing and Redevelopment Board, op. cit.,
p. 16.

8. Letter to Miss Mildred Zucker of Franklin
Plaza Housing Company from Martin Schneider, Public
Relations Consultant, Victor Weingarten Company, Inc.,
September 6, 1963.

9. Ibid.

4

CHARACTERISTICS
OF THE
SAMPLE
POPULATION

The Field Survey Instrument used in this study consisted of three sections providing three bodies of data for this study: general characteristics of all groups interviewed, information pertaining to the social variables necessary to test the major hypotheses of the study and information regarding general attitudes toward cooperative and rental tenure. This last section consisted of two separate parts, divided according to tenure. The cooperative housing respondents were questioned on their attitudes toward cooperative ownership, while the questions administered to the public housing respondents centered upon their attitudes toward public rental housing, as well as their attitudes and aspirations toward cooperative ownership. This last section of the research instrument and the data collected are discussed in Chapter 8.

THE SAMPLE

The households to be interviewed were sampled from three different population groups, drawn from three housing developments in East Harlem:

Group 1--fifty families living in a moderate-income cooperative housing development (Franklin Plaza)

Group 2--fifty families living in a moderate-

income rental public housing project
(Lexington Houses)

Group 3--fifty families living in a low-income
        rental public housing project (Jefferson
        Houses).

Each group was distinct from one another--with
respect to tenure in the case of the moderate-income
Franklin Plaza and Lexington groups and with respect
to income in the case of the Jefferson group. From
each of the housing developments, a sample of fifty
was drawn and was stratified according to household
composition. Eighty percent of the households
interviewed had at least one school-age child, while
the remaining 20 percent of those interviewed were
childless couples and single people, for the most
part, over sixty years old. The majority of childless
households lived in one-bedroom apartments in all of
the developments surveyed.

It is to be noted that these proportions were
chosen with the aim of including what was felt to
be a ratio representative of the household composition usually found in high-rise multiple-dwellings
in areas such as East Harlem. Housing agency policy
does not allow children to share a bedroom with
adult members of a household in municipally administered housing developments, and, thus, families with
children are not permitted to live in apartments
smaller than two-bedroom units. Also, childless
couples are not allowed to rent apartments with more
than one bedroom. Only at Franklin Plaza was this
regulation waived to any extent; childless couples
were occasionally allowed to rent two-bedroom
apartments. These households were rejected from
the sample through the use of an introductory question
in the interview schedule asking residents: "Are
there any school-age children living in this apartment?" Respondents in two-bedroom apartments who
did not have children were immediately eliminated
from the sample. This screening question was inverted
for residents of one-bedroom apartments.

In this manner, the sample was matched in all

three housing developments with regard to household
composition. Standardized floor plans for each
building in the various complexes facilitated the
sampling procedure, and each interviewer was made
aware of the floor plan for each building. The
resultant sample consisted of a total of fifty
interviews per housing development. To attain random
distribution in each of the buildings that were
surveyed, a table of random numbers was used to
select the apartments whose residents were to be
interviewed.

GENERAL CHARACTERISTICS

Household Composition

The households were selected within the sampling
procedure by household size and composition. A total
of 150 households were selected, fifty in each of
the three housing developments. Forty households,
or 80 percent of each of the three samples, were to
have at least one minor residing in the apartment,
while the remaining ten respondents, or 20 percent
of the households, were to be childless. The purpose
of this division of the sample was to ensure that a
percentage of childless families would be included
in the general sample population. The data pertaining
to family composition included the size of the household, the number and ages of the children present
and the sex and relationship of each person living
in the household.

There were slight differences in household size
between Franklin Plaza and the public housing projects,
although not of statistical significance. Household
mean size was 3.2 persons per household at Franklin
Plaza, 3.5 persons at Lexington and 3.3 persons at
Jefferson. Lexington household size was somewhat
larger than the East Harlem average of 3.2 persons
per household, while Franklin Plaza and Jefferson
were almost identical.

Family Structure

Data on family structure indicate that the low-income group had the largest number of female-headed households, significantly different at the .01 level from both moderate-income groups. Forty percent of the Jefferson sample consisted of households in which there was no adult male percent, in comparison to 20 percent at Franklin Plaza and 12 percent at Lexington (see Table 6).

Age of Household Members

There was no significant difference in the age level of either wives or husbands among the three groups. Although the Lexington and Jefferson groups had a somewhat larger number of husbands and wives between the ages of twenty to twenty-nine than the Franklin Plaza group, there was no statistical difference among the groups on this variable when age levels were clustered at a median point (see Table 7).

Racial and Ethnic Characteristics

At the completion of the interview, the race or ethnic background of the respondent was recorded. There was a similar percentage of Negro households in the moderate-income samples, 44 percent at Franklin and 46 percent at Lexington, in comparison to 24 percent in the low-income sample. Both Franklin Plaza and Jefferson groups contained a significantly larger percentage of white residents than did the Lexington group. The number of Puerto Rican residents in the Lexington Houses was proportionately higher than at Franklin Plaza. The Jefferson group, in turn, had an even higher number of Puerto Ricans than both moderate-income groups. In that there were differences along this variable between the moderate-income groups, its importance on the hypotheses being tested was examined in the analysis sections (see Table 8).

TABLE 6

Household Composition
and Family Structure
(By Mean Distribution and in Percent)

Composition and Structure	Moderate-Income Sample		Low-Income Sample
	Franklin[a]	Lexington[a]	Jefferson[a]
Mean Number of Persons in Household			
Total	3.60	3.54	3.26
Children	1.26	1.60	1.62
Sex of Head of Household (Percent):			
Male (Husband Present)	80	88	60
Female (Single, Widowed, Divorced and Separated)	20	12	40
Total	100	100	100
Marital Status (Percent):			
Married, Living Together	80	88	60
Widowed	6	--	20
Separated	2	8	16
Divorced	10	--	2
Single	2	4	2
Total	100	100	100

[a]Fifty households sampled in each housing development.

TABLE 7

Age of Household Members
(in Percent)

	Moderate-Income Sample		Low-Income Sample
Age	Franklin[a]	Lexington[a]	Jefferson[a]
Head of Household (Husband, if Present):			
20-29	4	14	18
30-39	32	28	36
40-49	26	18	16
50-65	26	34	18
65 and Over	12	6	12
Total	100	100	100
Wife (if Husband Is Present):			
20-29	14	20	20
30-39	28	22	22
40-49	20	14	12
50-65	16	28	4
65 and Over	4	4	2
Husband Not Present	18	12	40
Total	100	100	100
Children Living at Home:			
0-5	30	16	14
6-13	18	18	28
14 and Over	16	14	14
Combination of Above Three Categories	16	32	24
None	20	20	20
Total	100	100	100

[a]Fifty households sampled in each housing development.

TABLE 8

Racial and Ethnic Characteristics
of Sample Population
(In Percent)

Racial and Ethnic Background	Moderate-Income Sample		Low-Income Sample
	Franklin[a]	Lexington[a]	Jefferson[a]
White	22	6	22
Negro	44	46	24
Puerto Rican	30	46	54
Oriental	4	2	--
Total	100	100	100

[a]Fifty households sampled in each housing development.

The racial composition of Franklin Plaza in 1968 was significantly different from its composition in 1962, when the first residents moved in. One of the most important goals of the sponsors of the cooperative was to create a balanced, interracial community. Roger Starr notes that the first section of the cooperative contained an almost 50 percent white population.[1] The attrition of the original white population, as evidenced by this data and the general statistics on Franklin Plaza, indicate that the realization of this ambitious goal was short-lived.

SOCIOECONOMIC CHARACTERISTICS

Income

Each respondent was asked to indicate his income by choosing an appropriate category from an

income card handed to him by the interviewer. The
income level reported by the Franklin Plaza group
was higher in the aggregate than that of the Lexington
group. Seventy percent of Franklin respondents
indicated that their incomes fell in the $5,000-$9,000
category, in contrast to 56 percent of the Lexington
sample. Thirty-two percent of Lexington residents
reported that their income was under $5,000, in
contrast to 18 percent of the Franklin group. The
income level of the Jefferson sample was, as expected,
lower than the moderate-income groups. Eighty-four
percent of the Jefferson sample reported incomes
under the $5,000 level.

     In all public housing projects, income limita-
tions are imposed, and an annual review of reported
income is carried out by the New York City Housing
Authority. Although the income limitations in the
cooperative vary somewhat from those set by the
Housing Authority for its moderate-income rental
projects, almost all of the respondents in the
Lexington sample would have been eligible for Franklin
Plaza. It is highly possible that the incomes
reported by Lexington respondents were higher than
those indicated. Although this fact was not validated,
it is possible that, on the basis of aggregate income
data collected from moderate-income public housing
projects in New York City, the average income of
Lexington Houses was approximately $6,500, in compar-
ison to an approximate average income of $7,000 for
Franklin Plaza residents.[2] This might be explained
by the fact that many public housing tenants are
reluctant to report their actual income for fear of
having their monthly rent raised according to the
rent-income ratio established by the Housing Authority.
In that no significant relationship between income
and the variables being measured was found, it has
been assumed that both moderate-income groups are
comparable along the income variable (see Table 9).

Employment

     There was no significant difference in the
employment status of the male heads of household in

either of the moderate-income groups, nor was there
any significant difference between the low-income
sample and the moderate-income groups. Of the thirty
husbands present at Jefferson, twenty-seven were
employed, two were unemployed and one was retired
(see Table 10).

TABLE 9

Percentage Distribution of
Reported Annual Income
(In Percent)

Annual Income	Moderate-Income Sample		Low-Income Sample
	Franklin[a]	Lexington[a]	Jefferson[a]
Under $3,000	6	4	52
$3,000-$4,999	12	28	32
$5,000-$7,999	40	36	12
$8,000-$9,999	30	20	4
$10,000 and Over	8	4	--
Refusal	4	8	--
Total	100	100	100

[a]Fifty households sampled in each housing development.

The employment figures for wives indicated that
more women in the Lexington group were unemployed
(significant at the .05 level) than in either of
the other two groups. The fact that 44 percent of
Franklin Plaza wives were in the labor force, in
comparison to 28 percent at Lexington and 26 percent
at Jefferson would, also, partially explain the
higher aggregate income levels reported by the
Franklin respondents (see Table 10).

TABLE 10

Employment Status of Husband and Wife
(By Numerical Frequency)

Employment Status	Moderate-Income Sample		Low-Income Sample
	Franklin	Lexington	Jefferson
Husband:[a]	(n=41)	(n=44)	(n=30)
Employed	38	39	27
Unemployed	--	1	2
Disabled	2	2	--
Retired	1	2	1
Wife:	(n=49)	(n=50)	(n=13)
Employed	22	14	13
Unemployed[b]	22	34	28
Disabled	--	--	4
Retired	5	2	5
Not Present	1	--	--

[a]When present.
[b]Including housewives.

Occupation

The exact occupational status of each household
member in the labor force was recorded. Professionals
and those with managerial positions were combined
in this study as skilled workers. The semiskilled
category was used to refer to tradesmen and clerical
workers, and unskilled and service categories were
treated as separate and standard occupational
categories. There was a higher number of skilled
and professional male and female members of the
labor force in the Franklin Plaza group than at
Lexington Houses. However, when skilled and semiskilled categories were combined to represent high

occupational status, the two moderate-income groups
were similar (see Table 11).

TABLE 11

Occupation of Labor Force Members
(By Numerical Frequency)

Occupation	Moderate-Income Sample		Low-Income Sample
	Franklin	Lexington	Jefferson
Husband:	(n=38)	(n=39)	(n=27)
Skilled and Profes-			
sional	14	10	2
Semiskilled	15	20	11
Unskilled	2	--	5
Service	7	9	9
Wife:	(n=49)	(n=50)	(n=50)
Skilled	8	1	6
Semiskilled	5	7	2
Unskilled	--	--	1
Service	4	3	4
Housewife	20	31	20
Public Assistance,			
Social Security	8	5	17

There were only two male heads of household in
the Jefferson group who had skilled occupations, in
contrast to ten at Lexington and fourteen at Franklin.
In spite of the higher socioeconomic status of the
Lexington and Franklin Plaza groups, as compared
with the Jefferson group, the three groups were
almost similar in the number of men employed in
service occupations. This finding is probably best
explained by racial and ethnic factors rather than
income or level of education.

There was no significant difference among the
three groups in the occupational status of women

engaged in the labor force. However, there was a
much larger number of Jefferson women who received
their income solely from public assistance, either
from welfare payments or old-age pensions and social
security. This statistic would reflect the large
number of female-headed households among the low-
income group. There was no significant relationship
of this factor to the variables measured in the study
when examined by statistical analysis.

Educational Level

There were differences in the educational levels
of both husbands and wives among the three groups
(see Table 12). For example, four male household
members in the Franklin Plaza group were college
graduates, while there were no male college graduates
among the two public housing groups. Similarly,
only one Lexington male respondent received some
college education, in contrast to six male members
of the Franklin group. The differences among the
male educational levels were significant at the .05
level among the three groups.

There were even greater differences (significant
at the .01 level) in the educational levels of
female household members among the three groups.
Many more Franklin Plaza women attended some college
than did Lexington residents. Surprisingly, four
Jefferson women were reported to have had some
college education, in contrast to three Lexington
residents in this category. Only one Franklin Plaza
woman was in the category of having only some elementary school education, in contrast to ten women in
each public housing project. These data indicate
that educational attainment does vary among the
three housing developments, with greater similarity
between the public housing projects. Thus, some
of the differences found between the two types of
tenure may be attributed to differences in educational
levels. This factor will be examined in the analysis
sections.

TABLE 12

Educational Level of Husband and Wife
(By Numerical Frequency)

Educational Level	Moderate-Income Sample		Low-Income Sample
	Franklin	Lexington	Jefferson
Husband	(n=41)	(n=44)	(n=30)
College Graduate	4	--	--
Some College	6	1	--
High School Graduate	10	10	8
Some High School	4	8	5
Elementary School Graduate	10	15	7
Some Elementary School	2	7	9
No Formal Education	1	--	--
Unknown or Refusal	5	3	1
Wife	(n=49)	(n=50)	(n=50)
College Graduate	2	1	--
Some College	12	3	4
High School Graduate	17	19	14
Some High School	1	6	6
Elementary School Graduate	10	10	14
Some Elementary School	1	10	10
No Formal Education	--	--	--
Unknown or Refusal	7	1	2

Length of Residence

Few significant differences were exhibited by
the groups in length of residence in the housing
development or in apartment unit occupied, other
than those attributable to the length of time the
developments had been open. Very few persons had
lived in any of the developments for less than one
year. The majority of respondents from the public

housing projects had lived there for more than eight
years and, in the case of Franklin Plaza, since it
had been open. Few differences were found between
length of residence in the development and the
apartment unit itself. These data indicate that the
high mobility rate commonly found in areas like East
Harlem or presumed to exist among public housing
tenants is not characteristic of the sample groups
in this study (see Table 13).

TABLE 13

Length of Residence in
Housing Development
(In Percent)

	Moderate-Income Sample		Low-Income Sample
Length of Residence	Franklin[a]	Lexington[a]	Jefferson[a]
Less than 1 Year	2	4	6
1-3 Years	30	12	30
4-7 Years	68	34	8
8-19 Years	--	50	56
Total	100	100	100

[a]Fifty households sampled in each housing development.

Location and Type of Previous Residence

In both Franklin Plaza and Lexington Houses,
40 percent of the respondents had lived in East
Harlem before moving into these developments. At
Jefferson Houses, 60 percent of the residents were
from East Harlem. The high proportion of East Harlem
residents in all three projects was, partially, a
result of the aim of housing agencies to give preference to residents of the community in which a project
is built. Franklin Plaza had an active sales campaign

in East Harlem for a period of almost three years
to attract long-time white residents and the more
recent Puerto Ricans, who constituted a large proportion of the community. A sizable proportion of
Franklin Plaza residents were from Central Harlem,
almost all of them Negro. When Franklin Plaza was
built, there were few moderate-income housing developments in New York City that openly encouraged Negroes.
Long waiting lists for moderate-income public housing
and housing discrimination on a city-wide basis were
factors that would partially explain the reason for
the large numbers of Negroes who chose to purchase
cooperative apartments in a largely Puerto Rican
community.

There were no significant differences among
the three groups in the type of housing occupied
before moving into their present developments. The
largest number of respondents lived in apartments
before moving to these housing developments. Public
housing was the previous residence of 6 percent of
Franklin and Jefferson respondents and 10 percent
of Lexington respondents. This would seem to indicate
that Franklin Plaza had not attracted any significant
number of public housing tenants.

THE INTERVIEW PROCEDURE

The interviewing of residents was conducted
during a five-week period in March and April, 1968.
A contract was signed with a research firm in New
York City, which supplied professional interviewers,
primarily Negro and Puerto Rican, who were experienced
and familiar with East Harlem. The interviewers
were carefully instructed with regard to the interview
instrument and the sample design. Several briefing
sessions were conducted with the interviewers, and
a field supervisor from the research firm was assigned
to the study. In addition, detailed instructions
and information were provided on the interview
instrument itself (see Appendix). Permission to
conduct the interviews was arranged for Lexington
and Jefferson Houses through the New York City Housing
Authority and by the Management Office of Franklin
Plaza for that development.

The introduction to the formal interview consisted of the interviewer informing the respondent that he was conducting a study of housing in East Harlem for a "research firm" and that he was merely collecting general information. No mention was made of any relationship of this study to its university sponsor. In that way, it was felt that any preconception or bias that the respondent might have toward university research surveys would be eliminated.

THE INTERVIEW INSTRUMENT

The field instrument was developed in a way that would enable the analyst to ascertain the significance of the relationship between the independent variable of cooperative or rental tenure and the social phenomena being measured. In addition, the instrument provided a statistical profile of the characteristics of the sample population. It included general information on the socioeconomic and demographic characteristics of the respondents, their attitudes and opinions with regard to chosen social factors and their perceptions of these factors, as well as their reported behavior in relation to them. In addition to the questions on the instrument, observations from the interviewer, both specified and spontaneous, were used to develop an overall profile of the respondents.

THE SPECIFIC RESEARCH HYPOTHESES

The hypotheses tested in this study have been formulated on the basis of the background provided in the literature regarding the social effects attributed to cooperative tenure. This formulation, in turn, relies on logical deductions from the general proposition that, for this study's population, neighborly interaction, community solidarity, participation in community affairs and attitudes and feelings of pride toward the residential development are related to tenure.

These concepts have been well established in

the general theoretical literature on urbanism and
have been referred to, either directly or indirectly,
in the literature on tenure policy. A brief introduction to these concepts will provide a framework
for examining the hypotheses on which this study is
based. Neighborly interaction is viewed in terms
of socialization patterns within a residential
development. Community solidarity is an umbrella
concept, which includes such factors as group cohesiveness and identification, perception of group responsibility, satisfaction derived from residence in the
residential community and community spirit. Participation in community affairs refers to involvement
in the communal life of East Harlem, especially with
regard to neighborhood improvement. Pride in residence
and positive attitudes regarding the residential
development are self-explanatory. Detailed explanations of each of these concepts, as well as the
measures used to test them, are presented in the
chapters that follow. In summation, this study
seeks to examine existing concepts by the use of
established devices for measuring them. The hypotheses
thus formulated are as following:

> Hypothesis 1.   Respondents with cooperative
>   tenure will have higher levels
>   of neighborly interaction than
>   respondents of similar socio-
>   economic status with rental
>   tenure.
>
> Hypothesis 2.   Respondents with cooperative
>   tenure will have higher levels
>   of community solidarity than
>   respondents of similar socio-
>   economic status with rental
>   tenure.
>
> Hypothesis 3.   Respondents with cooperative
>   tenure will have higher levels
>   of participation in community
>   affairs than respondents of
>   similar socioeconomic status
>   with rental tenure.

Hypothesis 4.   Respondents with cooperative tenure will express more positive attitudes and stronger feelings of pride toward their home and residential development than respondents of similar socio-economic status with rental tenure.

Taken together, these hypotheses lead to the prediction that cooperative tenure is related to more positive social effects than rental tenure. A sample of low-income families was included in this study in order to determine the importance of socio-economic variables, particularly income, to the social phenomena being tested.

METHODOLOGY REFERENCES

One of the conditions of testing hypotheses is the constancy of the basic socioeconomic and demo-graphic factors. In this study, every effort was made to find equally matched groups. Mention must be made to the inherent problems associated with any research attempt to analyze social phenomena in an aggregate framework rather than on an individual reference framework. In spite of the use of personal interviews in this study, the analysis and evaluation of the data collected utilize the sum populations for the most part. The basic problem with research of this nature lies in the collective grouping of findings and generalizing from these findings for all individuals residing in the particular housing developments being studied.

Recognizing the potential shortcomings in this approach, a defense can be made on its behalf. Whether or not the individual traits of residents are uniformly similar to the average of the total population studied, it is relevant from an academic point of view to draw inferences on the total popula-tion of a residential development. The rationaliza-tion for this approach is based on previous studies of methodology that have clearly stated that the common socioeconomic characteristics shared by residents within housing developments of the type studied here provides a sociologically relevant framework from which to draw inferences.[3]

The statistical computation techniques used in this study are standard in housing research studies, and only a brief outline of them will be presented. The collected data will be examined to determine the relationship between pairs of variables in the various distributions and to test the level of significance of these findings. These distributions are presented in table in the chapters that follow. For purposes of reporting an estimation of the coefficient of correlation, the phi coefficient can be interpreted as a coefficient of correlation whenever the assumption is not unreasonable that the dichotomies being tested are actually variables that are normally distributed and linearly related, if indeed any relationship exists.[4] It should be noted that even when the phi coefficient is to be interpreted as a coefficient of correlation, it is still considered to be an underestimate of the correlation. It, therefore, was necessary to adjust the phi coefficient according to a table for converting phi coefficients. This adjustment was done to provide a more meaningful measure of the degree of related magnitude of association between the variables tested.

The chi-square technique was used "to test the significance of the differences between the 'observed' frequency distribution and the frequency distribution 'expected.'"[5] Only those data whose values are significant at the .05 level or less will be used to explain the reduction of the variation between dependent and independent variables.*

———————————

*For large random samples drawn from normally distributed populations, a chi-square distribution can be generated by the formula:

$$\chi^2 = \sum_{i=1}^{n} \left(\frac{X_i - u}{\sigma} \right)^2$$

To complete the profile of the study area in which this research was undertaken, a brief description of the three developments studied is presented.

SUMMARY

This chapter represents the attempt made to select two study groups matched on basic variables but differing in tenure. All the variables described in this chapter were selected for analysis in order to determine the relative degrees of comparability between the study groups. Aside from the expected differences between the low-income sample and the combined moderate-income samples, the moderate-income groups were relatively comparable in almost all variables. Some differences were found in the variables of household size, education and income, and these variables were emphasized in the analyses that follow. Although the moderate-income study groups were not perfectly matched, their comparability outweighed the differences that existed between them, therefore permitting the independent variable, tenure, to be examined from a relatively unbiased perspective.

NOTES

1. Roger Starr, The Living End: The City and Its Critics (New York: Coward-McCann, Inc., 1966), p. 104.

2. New York City Housing Authority, "1967 Guide to Housing Developments," (New York: New York City Housing Authority, 1967), p. 4.

3. Paul F. Lazarsfeld and Allan H. Barton, "Qualitative Measurement in the Social Sciences: Classification, Typologies, and Indices," in D. Lerner and H. D. Lasswell, eds., The Policy Sciences (Stanford, Calif.: Stanford University Press, 1951) pp. 187-92.

4. James E. Wert, Charles O. Neidt, and J.

Stanley Ahmann, <u>Statistical Methods in Educational and Psychological Research</u> (New York: Appleton-Century-Crofts, Inc., 1954), p. 302.

    5. Lillian Cohen, <u>Statistical Methods for Social Scientists</u> (Englewood Cliffs, N.J.: Prentice-Hall, Inc., 1954), p. 125.

5

THE SOCIAL
ENVIRONMENT:
ANALYSIS OF
NEIGHBORLY
INTERACTION

Research in housing and city planning has long been concerned with the study of neighborly inter- action in urban communities. A sizable body of literature has been developed on the subject, and the study of neighboring is considered to be one of the most important areas of urban research and community development. The relationship between tenure and neighborly interaction has been studied, although not to the same extent as such factors as spatial form and socioeconomic status. Most studies that include a measure of either direct or indirect effects of tenure on neighboring show that single- family homeowners in middle-class areas have higher scores in measurements of neighborly interaction than do those who rent in these areas.[1]

However, when neighboring is studied in lower- class communities, the tenure variable is not shown to be statistically significant.[2] Studies that focus on neighboring in low-income and moderate-income urban areas show that neighborly interaction is dependent upon conditions facilitating interaction and communication between people. As in suburban areas, neighborly interaction is possible when individuals are able to communicate with one another with relative ease. While social communication is greatly facilitated in spatially defined blocks of tenements, such as those described in the studies noted, it has been found that residents of high-rise apartment buildings, in particular, public housing, do not have the same avenues of communication open to them. Those studies that have analyzed neighborly interaction in public housing projects have concluded that there has been a breakdown of the traditional neighborly interaction patterns that characterized the tenement blocks from which most of the residents came.[3] The assumed relationship between residence in a project and the disintegration of neighborly interaction has been most important in bringing about a reexamination of the program's social results. In spite of an equally large body of literature questioning many of the assumed relationships between factors of public housing and disintegration of social interaction,[4] the negative research on the subject dominates. The irony of this situation, as was stated earlier, is that no serious research has been completed in public housing projects whose management and tenant-selection procedures are different from the stereotyped low-income public housing project. By studying a moderate-income public housing project, such as the Lexington Houses, it is hoped that a major contribution will be made to the literature on the subject, not only in contrasting the social effects of tenure policy but, also, in providing an empirically based analysis of the social structure of this form of public housing.

The same irony is present in the literature regarding cooperative tenure and its relationship to social interaction, in that no research has been completed that finds empirically that neighborly interaction is greater in cooperatives than in rental housing, and yet, statements are made as if on the basis of empirical research. One such example is found in a recent work of Albert Mayer. Without citing the source of his comparative data, Mayer notes "the enhanced opportunity for positive continuing social participation that being a cooperative owner-member in a development gives the citizen."[5] Unfortunately, no mention was made of the type of cooperative housing development observed, nor was any reference made to a comparative rental development.

The development of an atmosphere conducive to

neighboring is accepted in this study as an important
goal of community development and the cooperative
housing movement. The extent to which cooperative
owners exhibit a greater level of neighborly interaction than do tenants in the comparative rental
group is the hypothesis to be tested in this chapter.

NEIGHBORHOOD AND INTERACTION

     The literature cited points out that "neighborly
interaction" should not be confused with the more
commonly used term "neighborhood." The traditionally
applied definitions of "neighborhood" refer to a
spatially defined area, inhabited by a cluster of
families, with a sense of local identification and
unity. The generic origins of the term lie primarily
in the writings of Clarence Perry, James Dahir, and
Jessie Bernard. The extent to which neighborly
interaction occurs is described in terms of a
homogeneous population that is spatially organized
around common facilities and, for the most part,
composed of owners of single-family houses. The
conceptual literature ignores high-density urban
areas, which has led to the current popularity of
research oriented toward theory-building in an urban
setting.

     Although this study is not primarily concerned
with the development of neighborhood theory in terms
of spatial and population factors, both of these
must, of necessity, enter into a measure of social
interaction. To establish a framework from which
to analyze the interaction variable, the term
"neighborhood" has been accepted as the physical
setting where interaction takes place. The criteria
used to delineate its dimensions, however, vary
somewhat from traditional criteria. For purposes
of examining neighborly interaction, in this study,
each of the three housing developments has been
treated as a self-contained "neighborhood" within
the larger area of East Harlem. Three criteria were
used to justify this decision: (a) each housing
development is large enough in terms of population
to be considered as an individual neighborhood,

(b) each group of residents share common characteristics of housing, socioeconomic factors and racial
and ethnic backgrounds, and (c) the physical design
and spatial setting of each development distinguishes
it from the surrounding housing of East Harlem. All
three developments have institutions that characterize
the traditional neighborhood units described in the
theoretical literature, including neighborhood
recreation centers, meeting halls, public facilities
and representative organizations.

However, the measurement of neighborly interaction in these developments is functionally related
not only to the total residential complex of buildings
that comprise the development but, also, to the
individual buildings. Rather than focus on operational
definitions of the spatial concept and its relationship to interaction, the questions developed to
measure this variable are directed toward social
behavior in general. The spatial concept of neighboring is introduced only to clarify questions or
to evaluate neighborly interaction in terms other
than primary relationships. It must be added that
practical considerations and experience in the field,
rather than theoretical arguments, form the basis
for these decisions.

In treating each development as an individual
neighborhood, it was possible to study neighboring
in terms that are meaningful to residential developments not meeting the traditional characteristics
of the neighborhoods. This is especially relevant
to the understanding of neighborly interaction in
high-density urban communities, where conflicting
opinions exist regarding the subject. There is
impressive evidence that neighboring does exist in
urban areas.[6] That it is found in high-rise, low-
and moderate-income developments in an area like
East Harlem requires the introduction of new evidence,
particularly evidence that is based on the relationship between tenure and neighborly interaction.

MEASURES OF NEIGHBORLY INTERACTION

A Guttman-type scale developed by Joan Gordon

for a study of housing and neighborly interaction in Central Harlem was used in this study.[7] The Gordon scale is designed to report existing behavior rather than preferences and attitudes and is similar to scales used by many sociologists to measure social interaction.[8] The scale has been accepted as having face validity, and the responses have been coded according to a numerical range from zero to seven, with seven representing the highest score possible.

The use of scales of this type requires a word of explanation. Individuals may not care to admit involvement with their neighbors for fear of divulging information that might imply dependency and lack of self-reliance. This is especially true among minority group residents, who are sensitive to research that attempts to classify social behavior. Thus, some discrepancy may exist in the scoring of residents. To account for this possibility, questions pertaining to attitudes and perceptions were used in addition to the scale, in order to counterbalance whatever variance might be present.

The scoring of respondents in this study follows the rating schema developed by Gordon, but does not assign scores on an exponential basis as many Guttman-type scales do. In other words, a rating of seven is not assigned a weighted score but is scored as seven. The assignment of neighborly interaction scores relies on the reproducibility and validity of the pilot scale, and the ratings produced are treated as accurate indicators of the extent of this form of social behavior.

THE SOCIAL AMBIENCE

The reputed isolation and indifference of urban dwellers to their neighbors in their apartment houses has been given a sizable amount of attention, with little serious research on which to base the argument. To the same extreme, the literature on cooperative housing proposes that cooperative tenure is related to a more positive social environment,

in which neighborly interaction is common. It is
quite easy to accept the latter premise merely on
the basis of the efforts made on the part of cooperative housing organizations to encourage a neighborly
atmosphere.

In a recent study of integration in a cooperative
housing development in New York City, Harold Goldblatt
aptly summarizes these efforts in contrast to rental
housing:

> Few privately-owned multiple-dwellings
> provide common facilities such as community
> rooms, playrooms, laundry rooms, children's
> playgrounds where supervising adults and
> retired residents may also congregate, or
> the like . . . Few privately-owned multi-
> ple-dwellings, moreover, organize a system
> of hobby clubs exclusive to the apartment
> house in which the residents may join with
> their neighbors for their leisure time
> activities . . . In sum, to a much greater
> extent than the typical apartment house,
> the cooperative is a social organization
> of residents.[9]

The facilities described, as well as a similar
range of planned activities, are present at Franklin
Plaza, and it is true that they are rarely found in
privately owned apartment complexes in New York City.
However, the author did not mention the facilities
and social activities that are found in almost all
public housing projects in the city. Both Lexington
Houses and Jefferson Houses are virtually identical
to Franklin Plaza in the types of public facilities
provided. Lexington Houses has planned activities
for various age groups and interests, as does Jefferson Houses. Somehow, these facilities are almost
taken for granted in public housing, while, in cooperatives, they seem to be considered a result of
the cooperative way of life. At any rate, Franklin
Plaza, Lexington Houses and Jefferson Houses are
similar to the extent that facilities and planned
activities presumed to be conducive to neighborly
interaction are present. The questions to be answered

are: to what degree does neighboring actually take place; and to what degree is cooperative tenure related to this social phenomenon.

The extent to which respondents perceived a viable social environment was considered to be a significant indicator of this variable, and several questions were developed to examine evaluations of the social environment. Respondents were asked to rate the ease of making friends in their individual building and in the residential development. It was expected that the cooperative housing group would indicate that their form of housing was more conducive to friendship formation than the rental form.

There were no statistically significant differences between either moderate-income housing group, and only a slight variation in the distribution of responses by the low-income group (see Table 14) A similar percentage of moderate-income respondents reported that it was very easy to make friends in their building and in the development, although the intensity diminished in the latter.

These data would seem to indicate that the tenure variable was not a significant variable in explaining similarities and differences among the three housing developments. However, when these questions were correlated against the intervening socioeconomic and family characteristic variables, an interesting relationship was found to exist in the cooperative group with the education and occupational status variables.

A strong relationship was found to exist at Franklin Plaza between the ease of making friends and the level of education of both husband and wife. Significant at the .05 level for the male educational level and at the .01 level for female members, these data would indicate that while the overall social climate was perceived to be generally high, an even stronger perception of the ease of making friends existed among better-educated residents.

TABLE 14

Evaluation of the Social Environment
within the Housing Development
(In Percent)

Ease of Making Friends	Moderate-Income Sample		Low-Income Sample
	Franklin	Lexington	Jefferson
In the Building:	(n=50)	(n=50)	(n=50)
Very Easy	26	28	10
Easy	52	48	54
So-So	12	18	24
Difficult	8	4	12
Very Difficult	2	2	--
Total	100	100	100
In the Development:	(n=50)	(n=48)	(n=48)
Very easy	8	8	--
Easy	40	46	36
So-So	36	28	38
Difficult	12	12	14
Very Difficult	4	4	4
Never Try	--	2	8
Total	100	100	100

A similar relationship was found to exist at the .05 level when husband's occupation was correlated with the perception of the social environment. A significantly larger percentage of skilled workers perceived the social environment in more positive terms than did lesser-skilled workers. A similar distribution was noticed according to women's occupation, although this relationship was not acceptable as statistically significant. These relationships were found to exist only for the cooperative housing group, affirming the positive feelings exhibited in that development.

An additional dimension to the evaluation of

the social environment was provided by the addition
of questions relating to the willingness and ability
of respondents to recognize their fellow residents.
It was hoped that questions of this nature would
provide data related to the supposed indifference
and isolation of apartment dwellers and to the
expected uniqueness in cooperative tenure with regard
to this measure.

Respondents were asked to cite the number of
people in the development that they greeted when
meeting informally, along with the number of development residents that they were able to recognize in
a crowd, such as in a setting away from the development. There were no significant differences among
the three groups with regard to the basic social
formality of a spontaneous greeting in an informal
setting. However, a higher percentage of moderate-
income rental respondents asserted that they were
able to recognize most of the residents of their
development in a situation away from their developments. Tenure was not significant in explaining
these responses, nor were any of the intervening
socioeconomic variables (see Table 15).

While these questions are not especially refined
measures, the responses elicited seemed to imply
that each of the three housing developments provides
an environment that is, at least, conducive to social
interaction. Contrary to expectations, the tenure
variable was not a meaningful factor, and, in fact,
the comparative rental group's responses indicated
a slightly more positive evaluation of the social
environment in their public housing project. It
is interesting to note that there were no significant
differences between the low-income group and the
moderate-income group, implying that neither socioeconomic status nor type of housing is a major factor
in influencing an individual's perception of the
positive and negative aspects of the social environment. To further measure the dimensions of social
interaction, the Gordon Neighboring Scale was used
to evaluate the social environment from a behavioral
perspective.

TABLE 15

Recognition of Residents
in Housing Development
(In Percent)

Recognition of People	Moderate-Income Sample		Low-Income Sample
	Franklin[a]	Lexington[a]	Jefferson[a]
How Many People in the Development Greeted When Met:			
6 or More	78	80	70
5 or Less	22	20	30
Total	100	100	100
How Many People from the Development Recognized in a Crowd:			
Most	16	34	20
Many	42	24	34
Few	42	36	46
None	--	6	--
Total	100	100	100

T-Test X^2 = 12.73, df = 6, p < .05, ϕ = .08

[a]Fifty households sampled in each housing development.

THE NEIGHBORLY INTERACTION PROFILE

Level of Neighboring

The analysis of neighboring scores indicates that there were no statistically significant differences in neighboring between the moderate-income cooperative group and the moderate-income rental

group, thereby leading to the rejection of the
hypothesis that there is a relationship between
tenure and neighborly interaction. However, as is
shown in Table 16, there were significant differences
between the moderate-income sample and the low-income
sample at the .02 level,* implying that socioeconomic
factors rather than tenure are associated with the
variable measured. As is shown, the distribution
of scores for the two moderate-income groups were
similar, although the rental group had a slightly
higher mean score, 4.0, as compared to 3.46 for the
cooperative group.

There were no differences in the percentage
distribution of moderate-income respondents with
high neighboring scores: 26 percent of the cooperative
group and 24 percent of the rental group had high
scores. Only one respondent in the low-income group
achieved a high neighboring score, while 72 percent
of the respondents in that project scored at the
lowest level. While the significant differences
were found only by comparing the moderate-income
sample with the low-income sample, there were several
intergroup relationships between neighborly interaction
and the intervening socioeconomic and demographic
variables described in Chapter 4, which are useful
in dimensioning the profile of neighborly interaction.

---

*It was decided to use the T-test to examine
the intergroup relationships along the variable, as
well as the solidarity and participation scores.
The formula used was the following:

$$T = \frac{X_1 - X_2}{\sqrt{\left(\dfrac{N_1 N_2}{N_1 + N_2}\right)\dfrac{(N_1-1)\Delta_1^2 + (N_2-1)\Delta_2^2}{N_1 + N_2 - 2}}}$$

TABLE 16

Neighboring Scores
(In Percent)

Score	Moderate-Income Sample		Low-Income Sample
	Franklin[a]	Lexington[a]	Jefferson[a]
Neighboring Scores:			
Low (0-3)	50	40	72
Average (4-5)	24	36	26
High (6-7)	26	24	2
Total	100	100	100
T-Test X^2 = 5.47, df = 6, p < .02, ϕ = .24			
Mean Score	x̄ 3.46	x̄ 4.00	x̄ 2.44
Standard Deviation	s 2.32	s 1.77	s 1.62

[a]Fifty households sampled in each housing
development.

Variables Related to
Neighborly Interaction

The analysis of variables related to neighborly
interaction provides a meaningful perspective from
which to orient programs related to community development and urban housing. Negating the hypothesis
regarding the relationship of the tenure variable to
neighboring leaves only basic socioeconomic variables
and attitudes to examine.

Even though all of the following characteristics are interrelated and affect one another, they can be isolated and discussed separately for purposes of this study.

Number of Children

Only in the cooperative housing group was a relationship found between the number of children and higher scores of neighborly interaction. Although not statistically acceptable for this study, it would appear that the number of children in a household seems to be positively related to intensity of neighborly interaction, implying that children provide either added reasons or opportunities to interact in a face-to-face contact with development neighbors. However, since this relationship was not found to be especially significant nor present in the public housing samples, it would be invalid to present assumptions or hypotheses based on a relationship found to exist within only one housing development.

Education

It was expected that better-educated residents of the three housing developments would be more inclined to interact with neighbors than would lesser-educated individuals. It was further assumed that poorly educated persons lack the confidence, as well as the interest, needed to expand their social field beyond the immediate home environment. A relationship was found to exist in the Jefferson and Lexington housing projects along this variable, but not in Franklin Plaza. In both public housing groups, higher neighboring scores were found to be associated with higher levels of education for husbands and wives. This finding must be questioned in light of the fact that it did not hold true for the cooperative respondents.

Wife's Occupation

Women who were housewives received higher neighboring scores than did those who were employed.

This simply seems to imply that women who are at home rather than in the labor force have more of an opportunity, and, probably, more predilection, to interact with their neighbors than to those women whose daily schedule restricts intense neighborly interaction. There was no significant relationship found within the low-income sample, once more reflecting the relatively poor social environment in that project.

Aside from the variables mentioned, no significant relationships were found between neighborly interaction and such factors as age, employment status, marital status and length of residence. Only in the last variable, length of residence, do the findings of this study resemble the findings of more general studies of neighboring, in which evidence has been provided that neighborly interaction is not related to the time factor.[10]

SUMMARY

In recapitulating the findings in this chapter, the tenure variable was found to be of no significance in explaining variations in the intensity of neighborly interaction within two comparative groups of respondents. Aside from the rejection of the tenure variable, the major finding of this analysis is, simply, that low-income respondents are different than moderate-income respondents in their social behavior. This was not an unexpected finding by any means in view of the sizable body of completed research on the socialization patterns of low-income families in public housing. The fact that there were few relationships found to exist between interaction and basic socioeconomic and demographic variables would seem to imply that income level was the primary differentiating variable and not the more commonly believed variables such as those already mentioned.

It is surprising that neighborly interaction existed at the relatively high level reported for all three groups. In that residents of high-rise

apartment buildings are supposedly indifferent to
their neighbors, the findings of this study would
seem to indicate that neighborly interaction can
and does exist in what would appear to be a physical
environment nonconducive to such behavior. The
existence of neighborly interaction at the levels
found would also seem to question the premise often
made that apartment living inhibits neighborly
interaction. What might be offered instead is the
premise that income level, and, to a lesser extent,
education and number of children, are more important
factors than tenure in explaining the presence or
absence of neighboring.

NOTES

1. This finding was affirmed in a variety of
studies, including Donald L. Foley, "Neighbors or
Urbanites?" (Rochester, N.Y.: University of
Rochester, Department of Sociology, 1952); Ruth Hill
Useem, John Useem and Duane L. Gibson, "The Function
of Neighboring for the Middle Class Male," Human
Organization, XIX (Summer, 1960), 68-76. A socio-
metric study of the social cohesiveness of metropolitan neighborhoods in Minneapolis indicated that
single-family homeowners showed marked differences
in neighboring over apartment owners; Theodore Caplow
and Robert Forman, "Neighborhood Interaction in a
Homogeneous Community," American Sociological Review,
XV (June, 1950), 357-66. One of the earliest studies
of the supposed social disintegration caused by
apartment living was made by James S. Herman, Why
Do You Live in an Apartment: A Study of a Sinister
Trend in American Life (Detroit: Michigan Housing
Association, 1931), quoted in The President's
Conference on Home Building and Home Ownership,
Housing and the Community--Home Repair and Remodelling
(Washington, D.C.: Government Printing Office,
1932), pp. 95-103.

2. Some of the more important studies include
the following: Herbert J. Gans, The Urban Villagers
(New York: The Free Press, 1962); Marc Fried and
Peggy Gleicher, "Some Sources of Residential

Satisfaction in an Urban Slum," Journal of American Institute of Planners, XXVII, No. 4 (November, 1961), 305-15; and Edward T. Ryan, "Personal Identity in an Urban Slum," in Leonard J. Duhl, ed., The Urban Condition (New York: Basic Books, Inc., 1963), pp. 135-50.

3. See, especially, Marc Fried, "Grieving for a Lost Home," in Duhl, ed., op. cit., pp. 131-71; Chester Hartman, "The Housing of Relocated Families," Journal of the American Institute of Planners, XXX (November, 1964), 266-86; Herbert J. Gans, "The Human Implications of Current Redevelopment and Relocation Planning," Journal of the American Institute of Planners, XXV (February, 1959), 15-25.

4. The assumed correlation between public housing and the absence of social participation is challenged by Robert K. Merton in his article "The Social Psychology of Housing," in Wayne Dennis, ed., Current Trends in Social Psychology (Pittsburgh, Pa.: University of Pittsburgh Press, 1948), pp. 163-188. Merton argues that "the folkphrase that 'public housing projects' do or do not promote social participation is not a proposition in the sciences of social psychology or sociology. Nor does the finding provide clues to the distinctive complex of variables, masked by the blanket term 'public housing projects' which are related to social participation."

5. Albert Mayer, The Urgent Future (New York: McGraw-Hill Book Company, 1967), p. 64.

6. In a composite review of neighborly inter- action in metropolitan areas, in William M. Dobriner, ed., The Suburban Community (New York: Putnam's Sons, 1958), p. 128, the author notes: "Many recent studies have already begun to show that neighboring is more common in cities than had been expected. It appears that the seeds of local intimacy have already been planted in much of the urban population." It will be interesting to determine in this study the extent to which cooperative ownership nurtures the "seeds" referred to by Dobriner.

7. Joan Gorden, "The Poor of Harlem: Social
Functioning in the Underclass" (New York: Office
of the Mayor, Interdepartmental Neighborhood Service
Center, 1965). The coefficient of reproducibility
reported in her study was 94.51.

8. See, among others, Theodore Caplow and
Robert Forman, "Neighboring Interaction in a
Homogeneous Community," American Sociological Review,
XV (June, 1950), 357-66; Joel Smith, William H. Form
and Gregory P. Stone, "Local Intimacy in a Middle-
Size City," American Journal of Sociology, XV
(November, 1954), 276-84; and Paul Wallin, "A Guttman
Scale for Measuring Women's Neighborliness," American
Journal of Sociology, LIX (November, 1953), 241-46.

9. Harold Goldblatt, "Residential Stability in
an Integrated Middle Income Cooperative" (Report
No. 15; New York: City of New York Commission on
Human Rights, 1964), p. 14.

10. See, among others, William H. Whyte, Jr.,
The Organization Man (New York: Simon and Schuster,
1956), pp. 295-96; Leon Festinger, "Architecture and
Group Membership," Journal of Social Issues, VII,
Nos. 1 and 2 (1951), 158 ff; and Eugene Litwak,
"Reference Group Theory, Bureaucratic Career, and
Neighborhood Primary Group Cohesion," Sociometry,
XXIII (March, 1960), 72-84.

6

Basic to socially oriented housing policy is the need to create cohesive communities and to encourage residents to work together as a group toward this goal. Ideally, the residents of a cooperatively owned housing development should function as members of an interdependent social group, which possesses its own set of values and shared norms of behavior. Cooperative owners should not only identify with the cooperative in terms of pride in residence but should also identify with those principles of cooperative living that stress group cohesiveness and responsibility toward the cooperative. This total process is referred to in this study as "community solidarity"; it shares many of the premises of the theory of mutualism, which advocates a social organization, based on common ownership, which fosters common effort and control, and regulated by sentiments of mutual help and brotherhood.

Community solidarity is defined as the integra- tion or cohesiveness of residents of a housing development. Solidarity is examined as a group property, concerning both the mutual positive atti- tudes toward the total residential community and the particular aspects of group behavior or process.[1] Given the basic factors of cohesiveness or integra- tion as a group property, the concept describes the underlying philosophy associated with current housing

and planning policy aimed at community development
in urban areas. In that this study arose out of a
theoretical debate over the effect of tenure on
these factors, the evaluation of community solidarity is one that will add a necessary dimension to
the undertaking.

This study seeks to examine the concept of
community solidarity from a somewhat broader perspective than that which has been defined in the
theoretical literature. In addition to the fundamental elements of cohsiveness and consensus with
regard to shared responsibility, this chapter will
focus on such related factors as community spirit,
responsibility for the physical maintenance of the
housing environment, group identification and feelings of pride and satisfaction related to the residential community. After establishing a general
theoretical framework from which to examine these
factors, each will be analyzed in relation to the
hypotheses being tested. As shown in the review of
the premises and assumptions of the cooperative
housing movement, there is a firm belief that these
values are generated and developed as a result of
cooperative tenure. Further, critics of rental
tenure claim that the very nature of renting dimin-
ishes feelings of community solidarity, particularly
in public housing. The literature on both views is
extensive, although lacking in substantive, empirically based evidence, as was stated earlier.

THEORETICAL CONCEPTS OF
SOLIDARITY

The concept of community solidarity has its
roots in theoretical literature on community organization. Although most of the research on this
subject has taken place in the area of small group
research during the last twenty years, the concept
is important in the study of spatially organized
groups of residents of housing developments. This
was proved in Festinger, Schachter, and Back's study
of social behavior in which the concept was tested
in relation to social organization in a student

housing project.[2] The concept has direct relevance
to testing the hypotheses associated with cooperative
tenure, as well as to any residential environment
where distinct pressures exist to develop consensus
regarding behavioral norms. The proponents of cooperative housing argue that cooperative ownership of
property develops positive attitudes toward one's
residential environment. Apart from the feeling of
being part of a group or community, the two most
important attributes of solidarity are reflected in
what is termed "cohesiveness and responsibility
toward the community." It has been further postulated
that the residents of a cooperative are functionally
related, that is, they distinctively contribute to
the operation of the cooperative as a self-sufficient
system. Thus, it is important to determine the
degree of solidarity in a cooperative, in order to
determine the extent to which residents share a
common outlook, maintain effective communication and
share responsibility for maintaining the environmental
social order.

     For purposes of understanding the social effects
of cooperative housing, two major areas are involved
in the conceptual description and measurement of
solidarity. One area has to do with the perception
of the collective nature of the residents of a cooperative housing development in terms of cooperative
activities and collective action. This is ideally
expressed as a community or cooperative spirit
reflecting the residents conceptions of their neighbors. The second area centers about the particular
aspects of group behavior or process expressed,
primarily, in feelings of pride and responsibility
regarding the residential community. This latter
area is elementary to the success or failure of a
cooperatively organized housing development and one
that, theoretically, distinguishes this type of housing from rental housing. The extent to which the
overall concept of community solidarity, in particular, community spirit and collective responsibility,
is evident must be examined so as to distinguish
between hypothetical ideals and functional reality.

     Several salient points emerge from the literature

on community organization, which establish a framework
of analysis from which to examine the functional
reality of the concept of solidarity in the Franklin
Plaza Cooperative. In Jesse F. Steiner's classic
work on community organization, the solidarity of a
community is defined in terms of "overcoming the
forces of disorganization so as to hold the community
together, loyalty to common interests, pride in local
achievement, determination to improve community conditions, and willingness to cooperate for the common
good."[3] Although the concept of community solidarity
has been alluded to by professionals concerned with
housing policy and urban redevelopment, and its
absence has been much lamented by the critics of
public housing rental policy, relatively little
operationalization of the concept has emerged. Up
until Donald R. Fessler's development of a scale to
measure community solidarity,[4] most empirical work
centered about the consensus of urban residents as
expressed in attitudes toward crime and welfare
programs.[5] More recent studies on the community
have defined community solidarity in terms of identification with the community, interest and participation in the affairs of the community and sharing
of common values.[6]

What emerges from this theoretical framework is
the question as to whether those respondents having
cooperative tenure exhibit these many aspects of
community solidarity to the degree that they can be
differentiated from a comparative group of tenants
in rental housing. It was expected that the cooper-
ative-owners would not only score higher in the
overall measure of community solidarity but would
identify strongly with the cooperative in terms of
pride in residence, as well as in perceiving that
they are, indeed, unique and special as a social
group.

MEASURES OF COMMUNITY
SOLIDARITY

The conceptual complexity of the term "community
solidarity" required that several measures be used
to gather data pertinent to the components of the

TABLE 17

Community Solidarity Scores
(In Percent)

Score	Moderate-Income Sample		Low-Income Sample
	Franklin[a]	Lexington[a]	Jefferson[a]
Solidarity Score:			
Low (0-2)	2	--	12
Fair (3-5)	12	18	32
Average (6-8)	22	28	26
High (9-10)	64	54	30
Total	100	100	100

T-Test $X^2 = 20.51$, df = 6, $p < .01$, $\Phi = .07$

Mean Score	$\bar{x}$	$\bar{x}$	$\bar{x}$
	8.28	7.98	6.06
Standard Deviation	s	s	s
	1.99	2.08	2.79

[a]Fifty households sampled in each housing development.

concept. To test the hypothesis that cooperative tenure does foster greater degrees of community solidarity than does rental tenure for a comparable income group, a community solidarity index was used for the purpose of differentiating the sample members along this variable. Fessler's Community Solidarity Scale[7] was employed to assess the extent to which the respondent perceived the existence of community spirit in his development and to what extent the norms and values of group living regarding responsibility toward the development have been internalized by the residents. The Fessler scale is a ten-item scale, consisting of five statements related to community spirit and five related to responsibility toward the community. A score of one was given to every response that indicated a positive statement regarding the solidarity of the community. The range of scores for each respondent ran from zero to ten. The higher the score the respondent had, the more it indicated that he perceived that the development was cohesive and that its residents had internalized its norms and values. The scale was accepted at face validity. Although a split-half "r" was described by Fessler as being high, indicating the reliability of the scale, the exact statistic was not reported in the original research finding.

A total mean score and standard deviation of scores was computed for each sample. These scores are presented in Table 17. The average mean score indicates the degree to which residents of a development rate their development as fulfilling the dimensions of the items measured in the solidarity index. This score may be viewed as an index of the quality of community life that cannot be measured in terms of physical components alone. The score indicates, furthermore, whether the institutionalized social structure and processes of a residential community are relatively superior, insofar as they are scored high by its residents and relatively low when they are scored low by them. Thus, while the measure is called an index of community solidarity, it, actually, examines two factors: the residents' rating of the social behavior of their fellow residents, indicating the degree of community spirit that exists, and the degree of consensus existing in the community, especially with regard to shared responsibility for the residential development. Only in this latter sense, is it an index of solidarity in the traditional use of the term. In actuality, then, the standard deviation of the scores of all the residents for each development may be conceived as a statistical measure of the degree of consensus among these residents about their residential environment. The smaller the standard deviation, the more in agreement the people are, regardless of whether their opinions result in a high or low estimate of their residential community.

To measure the behavioral consequences of attitudes and perceptions of community solidarity, a
series of questions were developed to bridge the
hiatus between perceived reality and actuality.
These questions relate to the items measured by the
Fessler scale. In this manner, an added dimension
is introduced to the understanding of the concept of
solidarity, that is, the behavioral phenomenon of
action involvement, or the overt cooperative participation of residents, based on the mutuality or solidarity of attitudes and value consensus that they
hold as a social group. This behavioral measurement
is especially important, in that it assesses the
individual's view of the residential community, both
as a corporate unity and, also, in terms of his
role. Questions were developed to measure consensus
as to what has been, or is being, done by residents
of the housing development, or their formal organizations, to create a cohesive social environment.
Areas such as physical appearance and maintenance of
common property, group social activities by age
group and collective action based on group values
and goals are examined in terms of evaluation and
description of this behavior in regard to these
factors.

Before examining the scores attained on the
solidarity scale, a few words of introduction to the
evaluation of community spirit are necessary. In
this study, community spirit is defined in terms of
positive attitudes and resultant behavior that
reflects a consensus on the part of residents of a
housing development of the perception of group
cooperation and cohesiveness and of pride in residence,
or of norms and values regarding the physical maintenance of common property. In addition to the measurement of community spirit in the Fessler scale,
additional measures are provided in questions relating
to group cohesiveness. The analysis of the results
of these questions will follow the more detailed
components measured within the scale, so as to provide
a meaningful perspective for analysis.

LEVELS OF COMMUNITY SOLIDARITY

In evaluating the Fessler scale, no statistically significant difference was found between either of the moderate-income groups, thereby leading to the rejection of the hypothesis that cooperative tenure is related to higher levels of community solidarity as measured by this scale.* The scale sought to measure consensus of opinions regarding the residential community, as well as group responsibility toward the physical environment. Both cooperative owners and tenants in the comparative public housing project had, on the average, about the same consensus of opinion of their respective residential communities. The standard deviation of scores of the cooperative tenure group was slightly lower than that of the comparative rental group, but the difference was not significant.

However, as is shown in Table 17, the differences between the low-income group and the combined moderate-income groups are statistically significant at the .01 level, further supporting the rejection of the tenure hypothesis. This finding would imply that differences in these aspects of community solidarity are best explained by socioeconomic status rather than the hypothesized tenure variable. A possible inclusive explanation for this finding is that lower-income people do not relate to any meaningful extent to the larger community of a housing development but, instead, are more family centered or home oriented. It would appear that Jefferson respondents do not perceive themselves as being part of a community as a result of living in a housing project, nor do they perceive the existence of community spirit or consensus on the part of fellow residents regarding shared responsibility toward the residential community.

---

*T-test of association was used to test differences between each group.

Two possible explanations are offered for the absence of any significant explaining variables, other than the implied relationship between the socioeconomic level. First, the measures and relationships of solidarity were less defined than anticipated. Variations among the three housing developments at the high-solidarity level reflected fluctuations that may be attributed to limitations in the measure applied. Even more questionable are the results of the overviews relating to perception of solidarity. There is always the possibility that a "halo effect" could distort the data, in that residents attempt to rate their residential community in a good light simply because they presume that they are expected to do so. This explanation would probably best apply for the moderate-income sample, in view of the premise offered regarding the effect of role behavior. It was expected that there would be differences found along the control variables in relationship to solidarity. However, this expectation was not met, indicating that there was no significance with regard to these factors. These findings would further suggest that these aspects of community solidarity are not related to tenure in any more significant sense than variables such as age, race or length of residence. There were, however, some variations in the measure of community solidarity, when examined in greater detail than achieved by the scale. To evaluate the dimensions of solidarity, the items covered on the scale, as well as additional items related to the concept, will now be examined.

RESPONSIBILITY FOR PHYSICAL MAINTENANCE

Consensus on norms and values is an intrinsic element of the solidarity concept. The mutuality principle of cooperative living is presumed to instill active feelings of responsibility toward the maintenance of the physical environment, which are not found in public and private rental housing. The degree of consensus on this principle, or norm, of cooperative living is the variable measured in this section of the study.

To test the significance of tenure on this
variable, respondents were asked: "Do the people
try hard to see that the building is kept clean and
neat?" A significantly higher proportion of cooperative owners reported that their fellow residents do
try to see that the building is well maintained (see
Table 18). Significant at the .05 level, it was

TABLE 18

Group And Individual Responsibility
Regarding Physical Maintenance
(In Percent)

Query	Moderate-Income Sample		Low-Income Sample
	Franklin[a]	Lexington[a]	Jefferson[a]
Do People Try To See that the Building Is Kept Clean and Neat?			
Yes	74	60	54
Some Do, Some Don't	6	--	--
No	20	40	46
Total	100	100	100

T-Test X^2 = 12.93, df = 4, p < .05, ϕ = .04

Query	Moderate-Income Sample		Low-Income Sample
What is the Individual Action Regarding Vandalism of Common Property by Children?			
Intervene Immediately	76	62	54
Call Parents	6	12	6
Call the Manager	12	2	14
Do Nothing; Mind Own Business	6	22	24
Other	--	2	2
Total	100	100	100

[a]Fifty households in each housing development.

found that 74 percent of Franklin respondents perceived group responsibility to exist, in comparison to 60 percent of the Lexington group and an even lower 54 percent of the Jefferson group. A further measure of group responsibility was used to evaluate individual behavior regarding a hypothetical incident related to the physical maintenance of common property. To dimension the extent to which community solidarity has been incorporated into the personal behavior of residents, the following question was asked: "If you noticed children marking up the lobby of this building, what would you do?" More Franklin Plaza respondents indicated that they would immediately intervene and stop the hypothetical vandals on the spot than did respondents in the moderate-income comparison group or the low-income group. Only 6 percent of the cooperative respondents reported that they would mind their own business, in contrast to 22 percent of the moderate-income group and 24 percent of the low-income group. These findings would imply that a feeling of personal responsibility for communal property has been incorporated into the lives of residents with cooperative tenure. It would further imply that cooperative owners feel more secure about their personal safety and their ability to intervene without fear. A larger proportion of Lexington residents indicated that rather than stop the vandalism on the spot, they would report the incidence to the parents of the children. While showing a reluctance to intervene, on one hand, this response indirectly implies that they could recognize children by name. This fact is probably explained more by the smaller scale of the Lexington project, as well as by its long-time residents, than by the factors associated with social interaction, in that there was no significant difference among the groups along this variable.

Responsibility toward home maintenance is also considered to be a value instilled by cooperative tenure and purported to be lacking in public housing projects. To evaluate the reality of this premise, interviewers were instructed to rate the level of housekeeping at the completion of each interview. These data are presented in Table 19. The obvious

TABLE 19

Housekeeping Evaluation
By Interviewer
(In Percent)

Evaluation	Moderate-Income Sample		Low-Income Sample
	Franklin[a]	Lexington[a]	Jefferson[a]
Poor	2	6	4
Fair	20	34	34
Good	78	60	62
Total	100	100	100

[a]Fifty households sampled in each housing development.

biases or subjective feelings on the part of interviewers are crucial factors in collecting these data,
and an analysis of the significance of these ratings
must reflect the difficulties in attaining objectivity
with regard to this sensitive topic. Bearing this
in mind, it appears that cooperative owners are more
concerned with the physical maintenance of their
apartments than are public housing tenants. Although
not of any statistical significance, this evidence
seems to reaffirm the previous finding that cooperative tenure is related to stronger feelings of responsibility toward the physical maintenance of not only
the housing development but of the individual living
unit. It is interesting that the low-income group
had similar ratings on this variable with the moderate-income rental group implying that there are no
differences along this variable between public housing
tenants at two distinct levels of socioeconomic
status.

GROUP IDENTIFICATION

That people identify with a community is elementary to the development of a cohesive social

environment. The existence of "community" depends
upon the ability of individuals to conceive of themselves as being part of a physical and social environment that is apart from adjacent residential communities. These individuals, or residents, furthermore,
must identify with the community, both socially and
psychologically. The process of identification
might be termed "self-consciousness of community";
in this case, the perception of the interrelatedness
of the residents of this housing development.

It has been hypothesized that cooperative tenure
is related to greater levels of identification with
the residential community. Underlying this hypothesis
is the belief that the uniqueness of cooperative
housing results in strong feelings of identification
on the part of the cooperative owners with the cooperative development.[8]

Identification with a community is, by its very
nature, a complex process. Physical proximity or
similarity in socioeconomic status will not necessarily
cause residents to identify with their residential
community. Extrapolating, again, from community
organization principles, identification with a community implies that

> for a community to exist as a community
> and not merely as a collection of isolated
> family units, there must be agreement on
> certain matters. One of these is identi-
> fication with the community. People must
> feel that they belong to the same commu-
> nity . . . and that their individual fate
> is tied in with what happens to the com-
> munity. If they feel detached, if they
> lack this feeling of 'being in the same
> boat' with others, then one of the first
> ingredients of consensus is lacking.[9]

It is a goal of this study to examine whether cooperative tenure is conducive to a functioning consensus
based upon community identification. A corollary to
the development of internal interrelationships within
the cooperative is the process of establishing

participatory integration with the larger community,
which, in this study, is East Harlem. This latter
aspect of solidarity is analyzed in detail in Chapter
7.

When attitudes toward a residential community
cluster about a distinct core of values and common
social norms of behavior distinct from those held
by the larger community, community solidarity may be
assumed to be high; when opinions are disparate or
not unique to an individual residential community,
the community is not distinct as an entity, and
solidarity may be said to be lacking. One of the
conditions for community solidarity is the degree to
which residents identify with their fellow residents
and express preference to be associated with them.
The extent of group identity is best measured by
questions related to attitudes that influence personal
behavior. To examine the extent to which group
identity is related to identity with members of a
housing development, several attitudinal questions
were asked relating to the respondent's attitudes
comparing his fellow residents to those who are not
part of his residential environment. Respondents
were asked whether they felt more comfortable being
with people who live in the cooperative or project
or were they more comfortable with people in the
neighborhood, i.e., East Harlem. It was expected
that residents having cooperative tenure would indicate their preference to associate with residents
within the cooperative and not with residents of
East Harlem; residents of East Harlem are, for the
most part, at a lower socioeconomic level and possess
different values than the residents of the cooperative,
and, more importantly, group identity within the
cooperative was presumed to be at a significantly
high level to foster differentiation between cooperative owners and the residents of East Harlem.

Respondents were asked: "Do you think that the
people who live in the neighborhood are different
from the people who live here?" There were variations
among each of the three groups as to reported recognition of differences and the differences themselves.
More Franklin Plaza respondents perceived that the

residents of the cooperative were different from other East Harlem residents than did the comparative rental group (see Table 20). However, these differences become significant at the .05 level in

TABLE 20

Group Solidarity--
Perception of Group Identity
in Relation to Residents
of East Harlem
(By Numerical Frequency)

Query	Moderate-Income Sample		Low- Income Sample
	Franklin[a]	Lexington[a]	Jefferson[a]
Are There Differences Between Residents of Neighborhood and Housing Development?			
Yes	24	18	9
No	26	29	39
	--	3	2

T-Test $x^2 = 12.42$, df = 4, p < .05, ϕ = .04

What Are the Differences?			
Yes, Parents Control Children Here	--	3	--
Yes, People Are Cleaner Here	4	5	1
Yes, Wealthier Class of People Here	9	3	--
Yes, People Are Nicer, Friendlier and More Respectable Here	9	4	2
No, People Are the Same	14	17	31

TABLE 20 (Continued)

| Query | Moderate-Income Sample | | Low-Income Sample |
	Franklin[a]	Lexington[a]	Jefferson[a]
No, We're Just Lucky To Be Here	3	6	2
Don't Come into Contact with East Harlem People	6	4	5
People Are Better in Neighborhood than in Development	1	1	3
No Answer	4	7	6

T-Test $x^2 = 22.45$, df = 12, $p < .05$, $\phi = .05$

Do You Feel More Comfortable Being with Residents of the Development or with Neighborhood Residents?

Development Residents Only	21	17	8
Both	16	23	19
Neighborhood Residents Only	1	2	2
Doesn't Matter	10	8	20
No Answer	2	--	1

T-Test $x^2 = 23.33$, df = 8, $p < .01$, $\phi = .08$

Are Residents of the Housing Development Harder Working than Neighborhood Residents?

Yes	21	16	11
No	4	8	7
Same	24	25	23
No Answer	1	1	9

[a]Fifty households sampled in each housing development.

analyzing the distribution of responses among all three groups. A much smaller proportion of low-income respondents reported that there were differences between them and other East Harlem residents than did either of the moderate-income samples. These data, as well as the reasons reported for the existence or nonexistence of these differences, are also significant in evaluating group identification based on the differentiation function. The low-income group is similar in socioeconomic status to the residents of East Harlem who do not live in the Jefferson project, and a higher proportion of the Jefferson group were former residents of the community than were the residents of the moderate-income developments. In what is actually a heavily weighted question, it was surprising that as many respondents indicated that they perceived differences to exist, other than the difference in housing. Social and behavioral differences were perceived to exist by a higher proportion of cooperative respondents than did the cooperative rental group, although both groups were significantly different from the low-income group. Unexpected was the fact that several respondents in each housing development reported that they were just luckier to live in the housing development instead of a tenement in East Harlem.

The tenure variable was insignificant in explaining the evidence regarding specific attitudes toward residents of the East Harlem neighborhood. In comparison to only 16 percent of the low-income respondents, who stated that they felt more comfortable being with project residents than with neighborhood residents, 42 percent of Franklin respondents and 34 percent of the Lexington respondents indicated this attitude. Both moderate-income groups reported that they would prefer not to be associated with East Harlem residents, implying either strong internal cohesiveness, which would cause them to divert their social energy internally or, more likely, a class bias, based on the fact that their relative high status in an underprivileged neighborhood might possibly be threatened by association with East Harlem residents.

Only within the Lexington group was a correlation found to exist between husband's education and this attitudinal measure. It was found that, among those men who were educated beyond the tenth grade level, a correlation at the .01 level existed. No significance was found, however, when the education level of the wife was correlated against this variable. When the length of residence in the development was correlated against the differentiation measure, it was found that there was a relationship in all housing groups between respondents who had lived in the developments for a longer period of time than with respondents who had only lived in the development for a shorter time period.

There were no significant differences among respondents in judging themselves to be harder work-ing than East Harlem residents, although a larger proportion of cooperative residents saw themselves as being more industrious than did members of the Lexington or Jefferson groups. It is interesting that, only within the cooperative housing group, were racial characteristics found to be slightly related to the way this question was answered. A relationship was found to exist at the .05 level between Puerto Rican residents of Franklin Plaza and perception of the diligence of their fellow residents in comparison to East Harlem residents. White and Negro respondents reported that they saw no difference between the two populations.

GROUP COHESIVENESS AND COOPERATION

key element in community solidarity is the extent to which residents of a housing development perceive that efforts are made by either the residents, themselves, or the management to create an environ-ment conducive to group cohesiveness. The proponents of cooperative housing have indicated that this form of housing provides communal activities in proportions unmatched by public rental housing. It has already been stated that internal solidarity is a major aim of cooperative tenure and that a strong program of group activities and programs have been incorporated

into cooperative housing developments. Franklin
Plaza is no exception to this fact, as there are a
wide variety of planned group activities made available to residents. However, as few critics of
public housing seem to acknowledge, public housing
projects also contain an extensive program oriented
toward group cohesiveness. In the Lexington project
and the Jefferson project, tenant organizations were
active, project newspapers were published by the
residents and a full program of activities was available for tenants in the community centers and meeting
rooms incorporated into the project design.

The extent to which respondents perceived that
efforts were made toward the development of group
cohesiveness was taken to be an important indicator
of solidarity. An added dimension to this measure
was incorporated in questions asking whether respondents actually participated in these group activities.
In that Franklin Plaza residents are functionally
related as a group in terms of membership and participation in the management structure of the cooperative, in addition to the full range of group social
activities available to them, it was expected that
this group would perceive a higher level of cohesiveness to exist in that development, in contrast to
the comparative public housing group. Furthermore,
on the basis of these facts, it was expected that
they would participate in group activities to a
greater extent than would the cooperative group.

These expectations were vitiated by the evidence
that there were no significant differences between
the moderate-income groups or among the three groups
with regard to their perception of cohesiveness
within the respective housing developments. Over 80
percent of all respondents interviewed reported that
efforts toward cohesiveness were made for all age
groups within the housing developments. Few respondents perceived that their project or cooperative
was not conducive to group cohesiveness. Although a
slightly higher percentage of Franklin respondents
indicated that they perceived cohesiveness as being
encouraged, the difference was too small to be con-
sided significant.

When respondents were asked whether they participated in group-oriented activities within the
housing development, there were no differences between
either moderate-income group. However, there were
significant differences at the .05 level between the
moderate-income group and the low-income group.
Only 8 percent of the Jefferson respondents remarked
that they took part in group activities, in contrast
to 30 percent of the Franklin group and 26 percent of
of the Lexington group (see Table 21).

TABLE 21

Group Cohesiveness--
Participation In Group Activities
(In Percent)

| Query | Moderate-Income Sample | | Low-Income Sample |
	Franklin[a]	Lexington[a]	Jefferson[a]
Do You Attend Acti-vities in the Com-munity Center?			
Yes	30	26	8
No	70	74	92
Total	100	100	100

T-Test $x^2 = 8.18$, df = 2, $p < .05$, $\phi = .05$

[a]Fifty households sampled in each housing development.

These findings would seem to indicate that the
majority of respondents, regardless of tenure pattern,
are aware of the efforts being made in their housing
development toward the goal of group cohesiveness.
However, when the more important behavioral measure
is introduced, the moderate-income groups were similar in their level of group participation when compared to the low-income group, implying that socioeconomic factors, rather than tenure, were more

important in influencing this behavioral effect.

There were no significant differences in the
perception of group cooperation between the moderate-
income samples, once more discounting the tenure
variable in explaining differences in community
solidarity. Respondents were asked if people worked
together with other tenants to decide what was best
for the housing development. As is shown in Table
22, a lower proportion of low-income residents felt
that this cooperation did not exist in the Jefferson
project, in comparison to the moderate-income sample
groups, who perceived that cooperation was a basic
feature of their residential communities. Significant
at the .05 level, this relationship seems to imply
that group cohesiveness is present in these moderate-
income housing developments and, to a much lesser
extent, in the development populated by low-income
families.

Although tenant organizations, as well as
selected or appointed building captains and floor
leaders, are found in all three developments, few
low-income respondents recognized their existence,
in comparison to the much larger proportion of
moderate-income respondents affirming their presence.
It seems significant that low-income respondents
perceive group cooperation in terms of notices and
the project newspaper distributed to tenants, indicating that they do not participate in any formally
structured group organization. The opposite is
found in both moderate-income groups, who not only
acknowledged the effect of publications on the
development's cohesiveness but cited the formal
organizations as well.

A final indicator of group cohesiveness used in
this study is the perception of racial integration
within the residential development. It was felt
that, if the cooperative housing respondents recognized the integrated nature of their development,
this perception would provide a good indication of
the cohesiveness, which is presumed to be fostered
by cooperative tenure. Reviewing the racial characteristics of the three developments, Negroes

TABLE 22

Perception of Group Cooperation
in Housing Development
(By Numerical Frequency)

(a)

General Query

| Query | Moderate-Income Sample | | Low-Income Sample |
	Franklin[a]	Lexington[a]	Jefferson[a]
Do Residents Work Together?			
Yes	44	46	31
No	5	1	7
Don't Know	1	3	12

T-Test X^2 = 6.39, df = 2, $p < .05$, ϕ = .05

(b)

Detailed Query

| Query | Moderate-Income Sample | | | | Low-Income Sample | |
| | Franklin[a] | | Lexington[a] | | Jefferson[a] | |
	First Response	Second Response	First Response	Second Response	First Response	Second Response
How Is Type of Cooperation Perceived?						
As Tenants' Organizations	23	28	36	2	4	12
As Floor Captains and Building Leaders	9	4	7	9	2	1
As Housing Development Newspaper and Pamphlets	9	9	3	11	26	4
As Management Encouragement	1	2	--	5	--	--

aFifty households sampled in each housing development.

constitute about 60 percent of the population of the
Lexington Houses, 55 percent of Franklin Plaza and
33 percent of Jefferson Houses. White residents
constitute about 13 percent of the Lexington Houses,
20 percent of Franklin Plaza and 25 percent of Jefferson Houses, with Puerto Ricans comprising the remainder in all three developments. In no housing development was there a predominance of any racial group,
although there were more Negroes in both of the
moderate-income developments than in the low-income
project.

    Since racial integration was considered to be
one of the chief characteristics of Franklin Plaza,
it was expected that few respondents would perceive
the cooperative as being dominated by one racial
group. In that most people in housing developments
of this nature would be hesitant to admit that
integration did not exist, all respondents were
asked: "Is the project/co-op all Negro?" Surprisingly, the low-income group and not the cooperative
group asserted that their project was not all Negro
but was indeed integrated. As is shown in Table 23,
this relationship was found to be significant at the
.01 level, implying that a much higher percentage
of low-income respondents recognized the integrated
nature of their development. Although only one
Franklin Plaza respondent stated that the cooperative
was not well integrated, 30 percent of that group
reported that the project was all Negro, and an even
larger number, 38 percent, indicated that they had
no knowledge if this was true.

    It was expected that a question asking whether
a particular racial group predominated in a residential development, when, in fact, they did not, would
elicit strong negation. If cohesiveness in the
cooperative was as strong as implied, the respondents,
presumably, should have reflected their awareness
of integration, which is supposed to be one of the
values and goals of cooperative living in this
development. In that the responses were far from
expected, it would appear that either the question
was irrelevant to the concept of solidarity or that
a large proportion of moderate-income respondents,

TABLE 23

Perception of Racial Integration
(In Percent)

Query	Moderate-Income Sample		Low-Income Sample
	Franklin[a]	Lexington[a]	Jefferson[a]
Is the Project/Co-op All Negro?			
Yes	30	36	4
No	32	46	90
Don't Know	38	18	6
Total	100	100	100

T-Test X^2 = 23.85, df = 4, p < .01, ϕ = .10

Query	Moderate-Income Sample		Low-Income Sample
Is the Project/Co-op Well Integrated?			
Yes	74	56	94
No	2	6	2
Don't Know	24	38	4
Total	100	100	100

[a]Fifty households sampled in each housing
development.

regardless of tenure, actually did feel that they
lived in nonintegrated residential developments.
Even more significant is the large percentage of
moderate-income respondents who indicated that they
did not know whether their development was integrated,
implying a lack of knowledge of the basic composition
of their residential community. These responses
might also be attributed to the fact that many of
the white residents were elderly and not involved in
the development.

It was suggested earlier that satisfaction with
the project or cooperative as a place to live might
be related to the measure of solidarity of a community.

That is to say, if the residential environment does not happen to be particularly satisfactory for some individuals, they are more likely not to express feelings of community solidarity. To evaluate the relationship of housing satisfaction and pride in residence to community solidarity as a possible explanatory set of factors, the decision was made to include housing satisfaction in this section of the study rather than in the section on housing attitudes in Chapter 8.

PRIDE IN RESIDENCE AND HOUSING SATISFACTION

An important indicator of the community solidarity of the overall social environment of a residential development is the level of satisfaction expressed by its residents. Evaluation of housing satisfaction must be viewed from a multidimensional perspective, which includes not only measures of satisfaction with regard to specific elements of the physical environment but, also, with regard to elements of a more psychological nature related to living in a residential community. Earlier in this chapter, various components of the concept of community solidarity were examined, focusing, predominantly, on measures of the perception of the existence of group cohesiveness, identity and responsibility regarding the residential community. The index used to determine consensus of opinion regarding the solidarity of a community showed that consensus was similar for both moderate-income groups regarding the evaluation of the community spirit and acceptance of behavioral norms regarding the residential community.

Clearly, what is missing in this evolution of the conceptual elements of community solidarity is the measure of the levels of satisfaction and pride related to residence in either a cooperatively owned development or a rental development. In that pride in residence is considered to be the most important indication of housing satisfaction, this variable will be analyzed before analyzing the relationships existing with more general aspects of satisfaction.

Pride in Residence

It has been hypothesized that respondents having cooperative tenure have stronger feelings of pride in residence than do respondents having rental tenure. To test this hypothesis, respondents were asked: "Do you feel proud when you tell others that you live at Franklin Plaza/Lexington Houses/Jefferson Houses?" As is indicated in Table 24, there were

TABLE 24

Pride in Residence
(By Numerical Frequency)

| Query | Moderate-Income Sample | | Low-Income Sample |
	Franklin[a]	Lexington[a]	Jefferson[a]
Level of Pride in Housing Development:			
High	42	39	33
Low	7	7	15
No Answer	1	4	2

*One-Tailed Test of Association: $x^2 = \sum \frac{(O-E)^2}{(E)}$

T-Test $x^2 = 5.38$, df = 2, p < .05, $\phi = .037$

[a]Fifty households sampled in each housing development.

differences among the three groups, but these differences are only significant for the low-income group. Using the one-tailed test of association in order to assess the full dimensions of this variable, it was found that the differences between the moderate-income sample and the low-income sample were significant at the .05 level. These findings permit the rejection of the hypothesis that cooperative tenure is related to stronger feelings of pride in residence.

As was expected, a strong relationship was
found to exist between high levels of community
solidarity and pride in residence in all groups
surveyed. There were no significant relationships
found between the socioeconomic and demographic
intervening variables, except for education. This
variable was found to be statistically significant
for better-educated women respondents in the Lexington group, who indicated that they were not proud of
their residence there. This relationship was significant at the .05 level only for the Lexington group.
The husband's educational level was not found to be
significantly related to pride in residence.

An interesting relationship was found in the
cooperative tenure group regarding this variable.
There was a notable skewing in the direction of
negative attitudes toward East Harlem and high levels
of pride in residence, indicating that, while respondents were positive in terms of their housing development, they were negative in their attitudes regarding
the community. This relationship was significant at
the .05 level among the Franklin respondents, although
similar distributions were found in the Lexington
group, but not at a level of statistical significance.

It was assumed that if pride in residence was
as high as indicated, respondents would want to
share their residential environment with friends and
relatives. Respondents were asked if they had ever
tried to get relatives or friends to move into their
housing development. In both categories, Franklin
Plaza residents reported that they did recommend
residence in the cooperative to friends and relatives.
There was a linear relationship along both variables,
with 58 percent of the cooperative respondents
reporting that they recommended the cooperative to
their friends, as opposed to only 22 percent of the
low-income group and a somewhat higher 38 percent of
the Lexington sample (see Table 25). Significant at
the .01 level, these data seem to indicate that
cooperative residents have a higher sense of pride,
as well as level of satisfaction with this form of
housing, than the residents of public housing. A
similar distribution was evidenced in response to

TABLE 25

Recommending Housing to Friends and Relatives
(In Percent)

Query	Moderate-Income Sample Franklin[a]	Lexington[a]	Low-Income Sample Jefferson[a]
Have You Tried To Get Friends To Move into the Development?			
Yes	58	38	22
No	42	62	78
Total	100	100	100

T-Test x^2 = 13.16, df = 2, p < .01, ϕ = .09

Have You Tried To Get Relatives To Move into the Development?			
Yes	46	30	20
No	54	70	80
Total	100	100	100

T-Test x^2 = 7.90, df = 2, p < .05, ϕ = .05

[a]Fifty households sampled in each housing development.

the question regarding relatives. Significant at the .05 level, a higher proportion of Franklin Plaza respondents, again, indicated the positive feelings that they felt toward the cooperative.

Levels of Housing Satisfaction

Housing satisfaction is a difficult phenomenon to measure, and evaluation must largely rely on feelings expressed, either directly or indirectly.

To go beyond basic descriptive questions regarding
housing satisfaction, behavioral questions reflecting
housing satisfaction were incorporated into this
study. Respondents were asked what they thought of
their housing development as a place to live. It
was expected that a significantly larger proportion
of cooperative residents would be positive in their
evaluation than would residents of the comparative
rental group. However, as is shown in Table 26,
there were no significant differences between the
two study groups or among the three groups in total
terms of their evaluation, thus rejecting the relationship presumed to exist with regard to cooperative
tenure.

There was no significant difference among the
three groups with regard to levels of satisfaction
with their apartment. Whatever dissatisfaction was
expressed centered upon lack of space.

However, four Franklin Plaza respondents voiced
strong disfavor with a 15 percent increase in monthly
carrying charges proposed for Franklin Plaza. While
the apartments may have been highly satisfactory
prior to this announcement, these few respondents
were opposed to the increase proposed and voiced
their opinion to the interviewer that their apartments
were not worth the added cost. Although the proposed
rent increase was not popular with residents at
Franklin Plaza, nor in any of the Mitchell-Lama-
financed developments that also were to receive
increases, only a few respondents in Franklin Plaza
voiced harsh feelings or indicated that this increase
affected the variables measured in this study. On
the contrary, most respondents, while displeased
with any additional housing expense, viewed the
increase as inevitable and not unexpected in a city
where housing costs have increased at a rapid rate
over the past ten years.

It is both interesting and important for this
study that the reasons given for the positive evaluation of the housing environment were virtually alike
among the three groups. The clustering of responses
related to the physical attributes of cooperative and

TABLE 26

Evaluation of Residential Development
(In Percent)
(a)
General Evaluation

| Query | Moderate-Income Sample | | Low-Income Sample |
	Franklin[a]	Lexington[a]	Jefferson[a]
What Do You Think of the Development as a Place To Live?			
Excellent	6	10	10
Good	74	72	56
Fair	16	16	34
Bad	4	--	--
Very Bad	--	2	--
Total	100	100	100

(b)
Details of Evaluation
(By Numerical Frequency)

Details	Moderate-Income Sample				Low-Income Sample	
	Franklin		Lexington		Jefferson	
	First Response	Second Response	First Response	Second Response	First Response	Second Response
	(n=47)	(n=34)	(n=48)	(n=50)	(n=50)	(n=32)
Good maintenance; Clean, Safe	20	10	19	11	19	6
Cheap; Good Value	6	4	1	--	1	--
Nice Apartment	6	--	5	3	1	2
People Get Along Well	7	11	7	11	10	2
Convenient; Like Neighborhood	4	6	5	11	5	11
People Are Sloppy; Careless	1	--	--	2	3	--
Needs More Police; Safety Precautions	1	2	9	2	9	5
Poor Maintenance; Needs More Facilities	2	1	2	1	2	6

[a]Fifty households sampled.

public housing predominate, reflecting the importance placed on decent, safe housing in a community in which deteriorated housing predominates. More directly related to future policy is the emphasis placed by residents of public housing on the need for more police and safety precautions. It should be added that the Franklin Plaza cooperative has an elaborate protective system, including a sizable staff of private guards. Equally notable in explaining the relative unimportance placed on the need for more protection by Franklin Plaza residents is the fact that Franklin Plaza lobbies are locked at all times and can only be entered upon contacting the resident one is calling upon by the use of a buzzer-telephone system. This safety precaution is common throughout New York City in private rental housing and was one of the first improvements made in the conversion of Franklin Plaza from public housing. The installation of such safety precautions at a minimal cost proved to be one of the chief attractions in the sale of apartments. At the time of writing this study, public housing projects were still devoid of such safety devices, in spite of adamant demands on the part of tenants for the addition of more guards and the installation of a buzzer system in all lobbies.

THE CHOICE FACTOR AND
HOUSING SATISFACTION

Many of the criticisms of public housing focus upon the belief that public housing tenants are forced to live in projects that are not the choice of the individuals. The provision of alternative forms of housing, such as moderate-income cooperative housing, is viewed as one means of providing choice for families whose income and racial or ethnic back-ground limit their participation in the private housing market.

All respondents were asked whether the housing development that they lived in was their first choice of residence at the time when they originally decided to move from their previous residence. Only 54 percent of Franklin respondents and 46 percent of

Lexington respondents reported that these developments
were their first choice, in contrast to 74 percent
of the low-income respondents. Significant at the
.05 level, these findings seem to exhibit the well-
acknowledged fact that moderate-income families,
especially members of minority groups, were limited
as to their choice of housing and, more important,
residential neighborhood in New York City at the
time when these developments were constructed. It
is significant that such a large proportion of the
low-income sample reported that Jefferson Houses
was their first choice of residence, reflecting a
realistic appraisal of the virtually closed market
for families with marginal resources.

    Only the Lexington respondents indicated that
a public agency, in their case, the New York City
Housing Authority, chose their residence for them,
when asked: "Whose idea was it to move to Lexington
Houses?" In contrast to only one Franklin Plaza
respondent and two Jefferson respondents, who indicated that the choice of residence was made by a
municipal housing agency, fourteen Lexington respondents referred to the New York City Housing Authority
as the influencing force behind their choice of
residence in that project. The limited number of
vacancies in moderate-income public projects in the
city, coupled with the large waiting lists for these
developments, compels the Housing Authority to
announce vacancies only on the basis of availability
to applicants on the waiting list and not according
to preferred projects or neighborhoods. The critical
housing shortage at this market level not only bears
on the Authority but acts as a force directing applicants to accept the first apartment available, regardless of whether the apartment is in a project or
neighborhood of their first choice. The choice
factor was examined in relation to the variables
tested in this study but was found to be of no significance. This would also be borne out by the low
turnover rate reported, as well as the high levels
of satisfaction that most respondents, including a
large proportion of Lexington respondents, expressed
regarding their housing environment.

SUMMARY

The analysis of data presented in this chapter operated under the assumption that the consonance of attitudes and values with regard to the residential community is a worthwhile index of the positive functioning of such a community. All individuals rating high in the measures employed to analyze the components of the umbrella concept of solidarity were considered positively oriented toward the residential community, and their aggregate was taken to be an indicator of the solidarity to be found within the housing development.

There were no significant differences between the two moderate-income groups in their scores on the solidarity scale. The low-income housing project was evaluated by its residents at a significantly lower level than were either of the other two developments implying that this residential environment was inferior to the moderate-income cooperative and rental environments. The level of community spirit was rated on an equal level by both moderate-income groups and, at a lower level, by the low-income group.

In terms of group cohesiveness, both Franklin Plaza and Lexington respondents reported that this aspect of community solidarity was high. Participation in group activities was significantly higher in both moderate-income groups than in the low-income group. Surprisingly, the low-income respondents recognized the integrated nature of their development to a much greater extent than did either of the other two groups, indicating, perhaps, a greater awareness or concern for this aspect of residential living. Franklin Plaza respondents seemed to be more reluctant to socialize with people not living in the cooperative, indicating either a higher level of group cohesiveness than either of the public housing samples or, somewhat more likely, a reflection of a class bias that might exist between a relatively small cluster of moderate-income families living in a predominantly low-income district. Both moderate-income groups

indicated that they derived a somewhat greater
degree of satisfaction from their housing environment
than did the lower-income group, although the differences in evaluation were by no means significant.
The low-income group expressed lesser feelings of
pride in their residence than did either of the
moderate-income groups, regardless of tenure (statistically significant at the .05 level). What is
important for this study, however, is the enthusiasm
that Franklin Plaza respondents expressed with regard
to recommending the cooperative to friends and relatives. Similar findings were not discovered for
either public housing group, possibly indirectly
indicating that the measures of pride in residence
and housing satisfaction were not accurate. These
findings might also indicate an awareness of the
long waiting lists for apartments in public housing
and the difficulty experienced in being admitted to
public housing.

The major significant finding that distinguishes
respondents having cooperative tenure from the comparable rental tenure group was the consensus expressed
regarding group and individual responsibility toward
physical maintenance of communal property. Franklin
Plaza respondents perceived the existence of mutal
responsibility in a significantly higher percentage
than either of the public housing groups. While the
physical maintenance of all three developments was
generally good, Franklin Plaza respondents felt that
their neighbors were more concerned with maintenance
than was expressed by the other groups.

With regard to these findings, it would appear
that cooperative tenure is related to a more accurate
perception of its norms of mutual responsibility
and, to a lesser extent, group identification,
affirming this aspect of the overall solidarity
hypothesis. Within the context of this study, the
degree of community solidarity appears to be a function of an attitude-perception-behavior syndrome,
involving, among other things, stronger feelings of
cohesiveness and responsibility for the maintenance
of the physical environment. While these are important
effects that can be attributed to cooperative tenure,

more detailed research in the influence of management and the cooperative education program at Franklin Plaza must be undertaken before drawing any
final conclusions.

NOTES

1. Stanley Schacter, et al., "An Experimental
Study of Cohesiveness and Productivity," in Dorwin
Cartwright and A. Zander, eds., Group Dynamics:
Research and Theory (Evanston, Ill., Row, Peterson,
1960), p. 152.

2. Leon Festinger, S. Schachter and K. Back,
Social Pressures in Informal Groups (New York:
Harper and Row, 1950). The authors view solidarity
as being the result of all forces acting on members
to remain in the group.

3. Jesse F. Steiner, Community Organization
(New York: The Century Company, 1925), p. 101.

4. Donald R. Fessler, "The Development of a
Scale for Measuring Community Solidarity," Rural
Sociology, XVII (April, 1952), 144-52.

5. The most important of these studies is
Robert C. Angell, The Moral Integration of American
Cities (Chicago: University of Chicago Press, 1951).

6. Murray G. Ross, Community Organization:
Theory and Principles (New York: Harper and Brothers,
1955), p. 51.

7. Fessler, op. cit., pp. 144-52.

8. Jerry Voorhis, American Cooperatives (New
York: Harper Brothers, 1961), p. 46.

9. Irwin T. Sanders, The Community (New York:
The Ronald Press Company, 1958), p. 167.

7

PARTICIPATION
IN EAST HARLEM
COMMUNITY LIFE

Citizen participation in community activities is considered to be a vital goal in planning for stable and healthy communities and has been a subject of long standing interest in urban research. Research interest in the relationship between housing and participation in community activities stems from the belief that the characteristics of the housing environment, whether physical, social, economic or a combination of these, has a direct influence on the degree to which residents become involved in community-related activities. This belief is reiterated by Louis Wirth, when he states: "The degree to which people--individuals and families--find opportunities for participation in formal and informal organizations operating in the community is perhaps as good a test as any of the adequacy of housing."[1]

It has been hypothesized that respondents with cooperative tenure will be more actively involved in community activities than tenants of public rental housing of similar socioeconomic status. This hypothesized relationship implies that cooperatively owned housing provides an environment that influences its residents to identify not only with their own residential development but, also, is instrumental in fostering active participation in activities oriented toward the larger community of which they are members. The effect of both socioeconomic status and cooperative tenure will be examined within the context of this

chapter. In spite of the large number of studies
that show that community participation is positively
associated with socioeconomic status, none of these
studies has directly measured the effect of cooperative tenure on community involvement. The activities
in question relate to involvement in activities that
are focused largely on the improvement of conditions
in East Harlem. It is also assumed that a relationship exists between the degree of community solidarity
and the degree of participation in East Harlem activities. The premise for this assumption is that if
cooperative tenure is related to strong feelings of
community solidarity, as measured by community spirit
and responsibility toward the residential development,
this solidarity will lead to identification with the
activities of the larger community of East Harlem,
in that these activities are related to the well-being
of the cooperative itself.

Through the established internal participation
network developed in a cooperative, residents are
presumed to be well acquainted with the need for
active involvement in the decision-making process.
Whether or not the residents avail themselves of
the possibilities to participate in committee activity, they are, by and large, well aware of the fact
that

> as a democratic organization, the coopera-
> tive aims to develop maximum participation
> and continued interest on the part of its
> members . . . Members of a cooperative
> have a common goal of building a sound,
> strong cooperative. They strengthen this
> goal . . . by encouraging widest partici-
> pation by qualified members on committees,
> by working together.[2]

The importance of volunteer committees in
bridging the cooperative with the neighborhood in
which the cooperative is located is an important
function of committee work. In a report written by
Clara Fox of the New York Play Schools Association,
the author states:

> Volunteer committees are frequently the
> most constructive factor in converting the
> cooperative from a group of self-involved
> individuals into a group of community-
> oriented individuals. They give direction
> to the multisided affairs of the coopera-
> tive and relate to their neighbors with a
> high sense of social responsibility.[3]

One of the prime challenges faced by cooperatives,
especially Franklin Plaza, is to relate the cooperative and its residents to the surrounding community
in a meaningful and constructive way, as well as to
encourage community residents to relate to the cooperative. This is of special importance in an area
like East Harlem, which meets Fox's description of
an old neighborhood that often distrusts and eyes
cooperatives suspiciously.[4] If, indeed, the purpose
of cooperative housing is to provide a socially
viable residential environment in a healthy neighborhood, participation in activities concerning improvement is an important factor to be studied.

MEASURES OF COMMUNITY PARTICIPATION

The measure of community participation used in
this study was constructed by Delbert C. Miller and
is known as the Scoreboard for Community Services
Activity.[5] Derived from F. Stuart Chapin's Social
Participation Scale,[6] the Miller scale consists of
fifteen possible behavioral items that represent the
majority of activities related to community participation. Each positive response is given a weight of
one; the maximum score is fifteen, denoting an outstanding participant in community activities. This
measuring device rests on face validity; its reproducibility has been ascertained in the original
study conducted by Miller, as well as in a study
concerned with participation in relation to other
factors.[7]

The four components of the measure of participation in community affairs are the following: (a)
financial support, (b) general participation activity,

(c) awareness of community issues and problems, and (d) group action. The community referred to in this study is East Harlem. It was learned through pretesting that residents refer to East Harlem as "the neighborhood," and this term was used in the questionnaire. The interviewer was instructed as to the fact that this section of the questionnaire was related to East Harlem activities.

Before analyzing the results, it must be made clear that this score does not measure the intensity of effectiveness of participation but is limited to the amount or extent of the kinds of activity indicated. Additional questions were designed to evaluate the types of community activities in which residents of the housing developments participated, as well as the intensity of their participation. Data were also provided regarding attitudes toward East Harlem and its population, which will be discussed later in this chapter.

LEVELS OF COMMUNITY PARTICIPATION

The analysis of community participation scores indicate that there are no significant differences in participation between the moderate-income cooperative group or the moderate-income rental group, thereby leading to the rejection of the hypothesis that higher levels of community participation are related to cooperative tenure. However, as is indicated in Table 27, there are significant differences between the moderate-income sample and the low-income sample at the .05 level,* implying that socioeconomic factors rather than tenure are associated with lower levels of community participation for lower-income groups.

As is indicated, the distribution of scores for the two moderate-income groups is very similar,

---

*T-test was used to examine relationships between groups.

TABLE 27

Community Participation Scores
(In Percent)

Score	Moderate-Income Sample		Low-Income Sample
	Franklin[a]	Lexington[a]	Jefferson[a]
Participation Score:			
Low (0-3)	28	34	50
Average (4-7)	44	36	30
High (8-11)	16	22	14
Outstanding (12-15)	12	8	6
Total	100	100	100

T-Test $X^2 = 4.24$, $p < .05$, $\phi = .20$

Mean Score	$\bar{x}$ 6.22	$\bar{x}$ 5.90	$\bar{x}$ 4.70
Standard Deviation	s 3.69	s 3.57	s 3.54

[a]Fifty households sampled in each housing development.

although the mean score of the cooperative group is slightly higher than the comparative group's mean score, 6.22, compared to 5.90 for Lexington. In both instances, there is a distinct J curve, with the greater part of the population concentrated on the low end of the scale. Although a larger proportion of residents with cooperative tenure scored higher than did the comparative rental group, this difference was not found to be statistically different.

While the only significant intergroup difference existed between the moderate-income group and the low-income group, there were several intragroup

relationships that are useful in evaluating the
dimensions of community participation in areas similar
to East Harlem.

VARIABLES RELATED TO PARTICIPATION

Most studies of participation in low-income
neighborhoods show that scores are significantly
lower than are those of families and individuals in
higher-income neighborhoods.[8] The importance of
socioeconomic variables rather than tenure was found
to be particularly important in explaining the extent
of community participation by residents of various
housing developments in East Harlem.

The immediate issue with which this portion of
the research is concerned is to determine who parti-
cipates, and to what extent, in community affairs
and what factors are associated with such participation. In this manner, it is hoped that a complete
social profile of residents of cooperative and public
rental housing will be provided along the variable
of community participation. It was decided that the
reporting of trends, while not statistically significant, would be useful in providing a complete portrait
of participation.

Number of Children

A slight correlation was found to exist in both
public housing groups between the number of children
in the family and the level of community participation.
This relationship is most readily explained by the
fact that children provide a ready opportunity to
become involved in neighborhood school organizations,
such as the Parent-Teachers Association. No significance at any level was found to exist in the cooperative tenure group along this variable, although a
definite trend was evidenced.

Age and Race

It was expected that race and ethnic background,

as well as age, would be important influencing factors
with regard to participation. Significant at the
.05 level for the low-income group and at .10 for
both moderate-income groups, a relationship was found
to exist between proportionately lower levels of
participation for white residents, as compared to
Negro and Puerto Rican residents. This was especially
true in the Jefferson low-income project, where nine
out of eleven white residents had very low participation scores. While the factor of age is important
at any socioeconomic level, the racial factor appears
to be equally important. This is affirmed by the
fact that a higher proportion of white respondents
indicated that they perceived themselves as having
neither the ability nor the responsibility to improve
conditions in East Harlem. The elderly white residents
in the low- and moderate-income public projects also
perceived the decline of East Harlem to a much greater
extent than did Negro or Puerto Rican respondents of
the same age group.

Education

The supposition that participation is related
to education is borne out in the findings of the
study. As did Chapin's review of four experimental
studies of community participation, this study affirms
his finding that the larger the exposure in years to
formal education, the greater the subsequent community
involvement in terms of participation.[9] In all three
housing developments, regardless of tenure or income
level, the data showed a continuous and marked rise
in community participation scores with rise of education level. For the level of husband's education
and community participation, a relationship was found
to exist within the Lexington sample at the .01
level and at a lower level for the Franklin and
Jefferson groups. The relationship between the
wife's level of education and participation followed
a similar trend. Although not of high statistical
significance, it would appear on the basis of these
data that the relationship that exists between educational level and participation scores is relatively
simple and direct.

Length of Residence

No significant relationship was found to exist between length of residence in East Harlem and participation. However, a slight relationship was found to exist within the public housing groups between longer length of residence in development and participation. This latter relationship, while not of statistical significance, bears out the findings of previous studies of this variable, which have shown that individuals who are relatively new to a residential community are less likely to participate in community functions than those who have a longer history of residence.[10]

Family Characteristics

For each of the three developments, the community participation score and attendance at meetings was tabulated against marital status, age of children, size of household, employment status and occupation. Although other studies report relationships between community participation and these variables, this study found no consistent trends when making comparisons within each of the developments.

Community Participation and Neighboring

Several studies correlating community with neighborly interaction have concluded that a positive correlation exists.[11] While the findings of this study partially affirm those of the references cited, this relationship was only found significant for the moderate-income groups, both rental and cooperative tenure. The distribution of low neighboring scores was found to skew heavily toward the distribution of low scores in community participation. Significant at the .01 level for the Lexington group and at .05 for the Franklin group, these data seem to imply that those respondents who actively take part in social interaction within the project or cooperative are most likely to participated actively in community-oriented activities. No statistical significance was found to exist for this relationship within the low-income group, although similar trends were evidenced.

Community Participation and Solidarity

No relationship was found to exist between solidarity scores and participation scores, thereby rejecting the belief that group cohesiveness and responsibility would affect participation levels. It was presumed that solidarity would be related to community participation. In that no relationship was found, the question must be raised as to the adequacy of the measures used to evaluate community solidarity. Further research in this area would be useful for future studies of this nature.

CHARACTERISTICS OF ORGANIZATIONS
BY MEMBERSHIP

A comparison of active and inactive participation shows that participation tended to be concentrated in education-related activities for the public housing groups and, to a lesser extent, in community action programs for all groups. There were no statistically significant differences among the three housing developments, however, with regard to the types of community groups that respondents participated in. Participation in education-related activities was quite high for the low-income group, indicating the importance of the school for low-income families. In general, community participation was not very extensive for any groups, a common characteristic of citizens at both the low- and working-class level.

PERCEIVED ROLE AS INDIVIDUALS IN
EAST HARLEM

Although attitudes toward a community are potentially significant in affecting levels of participation, factors of self are also important and, in

most cases, more influential than attitudes in affecting behavior. Respondents were asked whether, as
individuals, they felt that they had the ability and
the responsibility to try to improve conditions in
East Harlem (see Table 28). Specific reference was
made to community services, such as schools or parks.
A significantly higher percentage of the moderate-
income rental group perceived themselves as able to
improve the community than did the cooperative tenure
group. As was expected, 48 percent of the low-income
group felt they were personally unable to effect
improvements in East Harlem, in contrast to 22 percent
of the Lexington group and 36 percent of the Franklin
group.

TABLE 28

Perception of Personal Ability and
Responsibility To Try To
Improve East Harlem
(In percent)

Perceptions	Moderate-Income Sample		Low-Income Sample
	Franklin[a]	Lexington[a]	Jefferson[a]
Perception of Individual Ability:			
Yes	64	74	52
No	36	22	48
Don't Know	--	4	--
Total	100	100	100

T-Test x^2 = 6.70, df = 2, p < .05, ϕ = .05

Perceptions			
Perception of Responsibility:			
Yes	94	84	86
No	6	16	14
Don't Know	--	--	--
Total	100	100	100

[a]Fifty households sampled in each housing development.

The question regarding responsibility was not successful as a measure of personal evaluation. There were no statistically significant differences among the three groups, although a higher proportion of the cooperative respondents acknowledged their responsibility to try to improve East Harlem than did either of the rental groups, perhaps reflecting their awareness of their role defined in the principles of cooperative housing, which stresses the importance of cooperative owners to be actively concerned with the community in which their development is located.

No association was found between these variables and basic social and demographic characteristics, implying that cooperative tenure is not associated with perceived ability to improve a community. However, a definite relationship was found to exist between perceived ability and activities in the community affairs. Those respondents who saw themselves as being able to improve East Harlem also ranked high in the community activity score. There were no differences between either of the moderate-income housing groups in that the significance level was .01 for both. The significance was lower within the Jefferson group, at the .05 level.

ATTITUDES REGARDING EAST HARLEM

As was shown in the analysis of group cohesiveness, a slightly higher proportion of Franklin Plaza residents perceived themselves to be different in several ways from their East Harlem neighbors. These differences were somewhat greater than those perceived to exist by the comparative rental group, but only significant in comparing the combined moderate-income sample with the low-income sample. The question arises as to what effect these perceived differences, which are thought or known to exist, influence attitudes and behavior regarding East Harlem. Clearly, if residents of the cooperative feel socially or even culturally apart from the community in which their housing development is located, it would seem to be unlikely that these residents would be willing to join in activities

that are community based. On the other hand, if
cooperative tenure is presumed to give its residents
a "stake in the community," then, these residents
would seemingly feel a need to participate in activities oriented toward the improvement of East Harlem.

Respondents were asked to express their opinions
of East Harlem as a place to live (see Table 29).

TABLE 29

Evaluation of East Harlem
(In Percent)

| Attitudes | Moderate-Income Sample | | Low-Income Sample |
	Franklin[a]	Lexington[a]	Jefferson[a]
Attitudes Regarding East Harlem:			
Positive	10	18	10
Indifferent	68	58	36
Negative	22	24	54
Total	100	100	100

T-Test X^2 = 16.29, df = 4, p < .01, ϕ = .05

[a]Fifty households sampled in each housing development.

The Franklin Plaza group was similar to the low-income
group positive attitudes regarding residency in East
Harlem, but different from the Lexington respondents.
Eighteen percent of the Lexington group viewed their
residency in East Harlem in positive terms, in contrast
to 10 percent of both the Franklin and Jefferson
groups. However, the differences among the three
groups become significant in terms of negative attitudes regarding East Harlem. While the Lexington
group evaluated East Harlem in slightly more positive
terms than the Franklin group, both groups were
similar in their negative evaluation, as well as

their expressed indifference to residency in East Harlem, in contrast to the much higher percentage of low-income negative responses. This might partially be explained by the fact that the neighborhood is not as important to families at this socioeconomic level as it is to lower-income residents, who are usually more dependent upon it from a functional point of view. This would seem to be further borne out by the fact that 68 percent of the Franklin group and 58 percent of the Lexington group were indifferent in terms of evaluating the community, in contrast to 36 percent of the low-income sample.

There were significant differences among the three groups when asked whether East Harlem had improved or deteriorated since their moving into the housing development (see Table 30). The Lexington group perceived East Harlem as having declined in significantly higher proportions than did the Franklin respondents. Significant at the .01 level, 54 percent

TABLE 30

Perception of Change in East Harlem
(In Percent)

| Type of Change | Moderate-Income Sample | | Low-Income Sample |
	Franklin[a]	Lexington[a]	Jefferson[a]
Type of Change Perceived in East Harlem:			
Decline	20	54	36
No Change	48	38	46
Improved	32	8	18
Total	100	100	100

T-Test X^2 = 16.77, df = 4, p < .01, ϕ = .06

[a]Fifty households sampled in each housing development.

of the moderate-income rental group reported the decline of East Harlem, in contrast to 20 percent of the cooperative respondents and 36 percent of the low-income group.

The cooperative tenure respondents were the only group to perceive improvements in East Harlem since moving into Franklin Plaza. Although major improvements have taken place in East Harlem since the mid-fifties, primarily in the form of new housing and schools, a large percentage of the residents of Lexington Houses and, to a lesser extent, at Jefferson Houses did not seem to recognize these as improvements. The public housing residents seemed to be more aware of an overall decline than of the efforts made at improving the community over the past decade. It would appear that Franklin Plaza respondents were satisfied with the efforts underway in the community, while the comparative Lexington group viewed the community from a historical perspective, primarily in terms of decline.

Although these attitudes were assumed to be important factors affecting levels of participation in the community, only the perceived ability variable was found to be significant when correlated with particular scores.

SUMMARY

What appeared to be a simple and direct relationship between tenure and community participation scores turns out, upon further breakdown of the data, to be a complex set of interrelationships, of which tenure is of no statistical significance in explaining the complexities of the interrelationships. Education, number of children, length of residence in development, race and neighboring scores tend to vary together, thereby producing a compound effect. It may, therefore, be reasserted that to attribute participation, as measured in this study, directly to the affect of tenure, or to education, race or, even, a combination of these factors, would not provide sufficient explanation.

One possible approach to explaining the higher level of participation among the moderate-income sample and the lower level for the low-income group would be to draw upon role behavior theory as a theoretical framework of analysis. The basic premise of role behavior theory is that social behavior is primarily learned behavior and is a function of the position the individual occupies in the social system. Participation in community-oriented affairs may be said to be a consequence of an individual's having a position in a social structure that calls for that kind of behavior.

Both moderate-income groups may be assumed to share the values of middle-class society toward which they are oriented. Participation is an accepted value and goal in middle-class culture; the more animistic culture of the poor does not place high values on participation in community affairs. While participation is a basic part of middle-class life, the Lexington and Franklin respondents are not yet fully a part of this class culture, thus calling for further explanation to evaluate the participation variable. The question arises as to what effect the internal social structure, imposed or developed in publicly administered projects or cooperatives at this income level, has on the level of participation in community affairs. What effect has the encourage- ment of group participation in tenants' organizations and cooperators' meetings had in instilling not only the importance of community participation in residents but, also, the skills and confidence necessary to become involved in East Harlem affairs? Furthermore, to what extent is community participation a function of being part of a relatively well-organized residen- tial development, where behavioral roles are ascribed by a set of external or formal forces and more subtle internal forces? The question must also be raised as to what effect the organizational efforts present in the low-income project had on those residents.

The commonly held notion that below-average- income residents, particularly those living in an urban slum, do not participate in community affairs must be modified in several details. Mirra

Komarovsky's study showed that a large segment of the general population, and, particularly, at the lower social and economic level, are not involved in community affairs and, in fact, are isolated from the formal knowledge needed to actively participate in community affairs.[12] Although there is no evidence in this study as to the differences in participation by low- or moderate-income residents of privately owned buildings in East Harlem and in publicly administered developments, the speculation is offered that community participation at this socioeconomic level is, partially, a function of the organizational residential environment.

The internal organization and communication and education network that exists in both moderate-income groups and, to a lesser extent, in the low-income project has been described earlier in this study. Community participation is a goal of public housing and the cooperative housing movement, and strong efforts are made to transfuse this goal into the behavioral norms of residents of these housing types. The ability or willingness of residents to accept this goal and incorporate it into their personal lives is, of course, dependent on a complex set of factors, with socioeconomic status being a key influencing variable.

On the basis of the significantly well-organized internal structure of both moderate-income developments and a lesser-organized low-income development, the premise is offered that this structure, regardless of the form of tenure, is associated with higher levels of community participation. The organizational structure found in these developments more than likely prepares people who, characteristically, are unable to perceive the relevancy of participation in community affairs through the development of skills and confidence necessary for community involvement. As was stated before, this process is a combination of tenant organization efforts, definition of both tenant rights and tenant responsibilities and the encouragement of a working relationship between management and tenants. The residents gain knowledge about procedure and means, as well as an acquaintance with the organizational structure and access to leadership. While social and economic factors remain important in the analysis of participation, the development of norms calling for, and encouraging, what might be termed "a spirit of community activism" can be initiated through a well-organized information, education and participatory program. The extent, as well as the importance, of such forces is a most important area of research, and it is one that should be stressed in future research efforts.

For a community like East Harlem, it was significant that participation in community affairs was as high as it was. Participation was not related to tenure but to more basic socioeconomic characteristics. The hypothesis that residents having cooperative tenure will participate in community affairs to a greater extent than will a comparative group having rental tenure was rejected. However, high levels of community participation were not randomly distributed throughout the population but were related to what may be considered some of the fundamental differentiating characteristics in our society. The lower-income sample was found to have a significantly lower level of participation in the community than did either of the study groups, reaffirming the importance of factors other than tenure with relation to participation.

NOTES

1. Louis Wirth, "Housing as a Field of Sociological Research," American Sociological Review, XII, (April, 1947), 140.

2. George Schecter, "How To Work with Committees," Cooperative Housing Quarterly, I, No. 2 (Summer, 1963), 17.

3. Clara Fox, "Volunteer Leadership in Cooperative Housing" (New York: New York Play Schools Association, 1960), p. 9.

4. Ibid., p. 18.

5.   Delbert C. Miller, Handbook of Research Design and Social Measurement (New York: David McKay Company, Inc., 1964), pp. 205-7.

6.   F. Stuart Chapin, Experimental Designs in Sociological Research (New York: Harper Brothers, 1955), Appendix B, pp. 275-77.

7.   Christian T. Jonassen, "Functional Unities in Eighty-Eight Community Systems," American Sociological Review, XXVI, (June, 1961), 399-407.

8.   One of the earliest and most important of these studies is F. Stuart Chapin's, "The Effects of Slum Clearance and Rehousing on Family and Community Relationships in Minneapolis," American Journal of Sociology, XLIII, (March, 1938), 744-63.

9.   F. Stuart Chapin, "Design for Social Experiments," American Sociological Review, III (December 1938), 786-800. See, also, Morris Axelrod, "Urban Structure and Social Participation," American Sociological Review, XXI (February, 1956), 13-18.

10. Robert C. Angell, "The Moral Integration of American Cities," American Journal of Sociology, LVII (July, 1951), Part 2, 119-20.

11. Among the most important are the following: Wendell Bell and Marion B. Boat, "Urban Neighborhoods and Informal Social Relations," American Journal of Sociology, LXII (January, 1957), 391-98; and William E. Barnett, "Neighborhood Groups: An Informal System of Communication," Rural Sociology, XIX (September, 1952), 371-73.

12. This area has been investigated in a number of studies, cf., e.g., Mirra Komarovsky, "The Voluntary Association of Urban Dwellers," American Sociological Review, XI (December, 1946), 686-98; William C. Mather, "Income and Social Participation," American Sociological Review, VI (June, 1941), 380-84.

8

HOUSING
ATTITUDES
AND
ASPIRATIONS

It was expected that the attitudes people expressed about their residential environment would be useful in determining the effects that a factor such as tenure has had on social behavior and community solidarity. In that this study has been concerned with the cooperative form of tenure and its effect on social behavior, it was important to determine the attitudes held by cooperative owners regarding their form of housing. It was also deemed important to measure the extent to which cooperative ownership has served as a model of aspiration and achievement for tenants in rental housing. Underlying this examination was the belief that owners of cooperative apartments would exhibit more positive attitudes toward their form of housing than would the comparable rental group. An analysis of the differences in attitudes among the groups would thus provide an added dimension to explain the differences among the groups along both the tenure and income levels. Besides evaluating general housing attitudes, the data presented in this chapter should offer valuable insights into the aspirations of public housing tenants regarding cooperative housing.

Franklin Plaza was presumed by many to be a symbolic element in the redevelopment of East Harlem and, even more important, a model of aspiration and self-status for residents of the community; it is important, therefore, to evaluate its effect on the

housing aspirations of the public housing group.
The interview instrument contained two sections
relating to housing attitudes and aspirations, the
first section was administered to the cooperative
housing sample and the second to the combined public
housing sample. Residents of the cooperative development were asked general evaluative questions regarding
their type of housing, as well as specified questions
about the financing of their equity investment and
about their attitudes toward a cooperative housing
program for East Harlem. Public housing tenants
were surveyed on their attitudes regarding public
housing, as well as their aspirations toward cooperative tenure. Both sets of questions are similar
in several aspects, and both relate to current
thinking in the field of housing regarding cooperative
tenure as a substitute for rental tenure. Specific
questions regarding Franklin Plaza were asked, in
addition to more general questions relating to tenure
policy.

As in other sections of the field instrument,
questions designed to record attitudinal responses
were of the open-ended form. After an attitudinal
question requiring either a positive or negative
reply, the respondents were asked to elaborate on
their reply. The interviewer was instructed to
elicit detailed answers from the respondents.
Responses were coded according to a range of categories
relevant to the attitude on housing being examined.
Although each respondent was encouraged to offer
more than one response to each open-ended question,
in many cases, only one response was offered. This
was especially significant for the low-income group
and for respondents of low education in all three
groups. In that responses were coded according to
general categories for computer processing, there
has been no distinction made according to individual
respondent as to whether one or two responses were
offered. As a result, it was possible to use only
raw frequency numbers for those categories that
predominate.

It is expected that the findings reported in
this chapter will have relevance for policy decisions

regarding housing tenure policy. Attitudinal
responses, particularly those responses that reflect
the aspirations of residents in low-income and
moderate-income public housing, are a good barometer
from which to base future policy decisions. Before
undertaking a change in public housing tenure policy,
it is hoped that whatever changes are proposed, they
reflect the needs and aspirations of those for whom
they are planned.

EVALUATION OF COOPERATIVE TENURE
AND RENTAL TENURE

     Cooperative ownership was a new form of tenure
for all but one of the households interviewed at
Franklin Plaza. As shown in Chapter 4, the majority
of Franklin respondents formerly rented apartments
before moving into this development. To determine
the attitudes influencing their choice of cooperative
tenure instead of rental tenure, respondents were
asked if cooperative housing offered a better way
of life than did renting. Eighty-two percent of
the respondents answered affirmatively, while 18
percent stated that cooperative housing was not a
better way of life than renting. The reasons given
for these answers are shown in Table 31.

     Among the advantages of cooperative housing
over rental housing cited, the responsibility of
residents to the cooperative and a voice in the
affairs of the cooperative were listed by residents
as primary. As was expected, the safety and cleanliness that Franklin Plaza offers its residents were
emphasized. Although eight people saw no difference,
the positive attributes of Franklin Plaza were widely
recognized. As was shown in the analysis of the
solidarity variable, cooperative residents recognized
the mutuality that existed in the cooperative. The
replies to this question imply that these positive
factors were perceived by the residents not to exist
in rental housing, or actually did not exist, in
previous experience with rental housing. The physical
benefits of Franklin Plaza as rated by the residents
were reported with relatively high frequency. The

uniqueness of a locked lobby and well-protected grounds in this particular development are interpreted by the respondents to be significant advantages over rental housing.

TABLE 31

Perceived Advantages of Cooperative
Housing over Rental Housing by
Franklin Plaza Respondents
(By Numerical Frequency)

Differences	First Responses	Second Responses[a]
Positive Differences:		
Residents are More Responsible	9	9
Voice in Decision-Making	6	7
Safer and Cleaner	8	12
Wealthier people, Better Class of People	2	1
Nicer Apartments	2	--
More Activities	1	1
Better Value in Co-op; Cheaper Housing	9	9
Negative Differences:		
Co-op Is More Expensive; No Other Difference	2	1
No Difference	8	1

[a]Percent with two responses, 74 percent.

FINANCIAL ASPECTS OF COOPERATIVE TENURE

One of the assumed principal benefits of cooperative housing for moderate-income families is that a cooperative apartment is a good investment. All too often, cooperative housing is equated with home

ownership in terms of its financial benefits. The
financial complexities of cooperative housing are
difficult for the professional to fully comprehend,
not to mention the typical resident of moderate-
income cooperative developments. The argument that
cooperative housing is a "good investment" is taken
by many to mean that monthly payments can be equated
to a type of "savings," since property is held in
common by all the residents. The fact that a down
payment was made further augments the belief that
savings are being accrued and that one's investment
is not only real but growing.

The savings under cooperative housing result,
primarily, from favorable financing and long-term
mortgages. Consequently, the charges for rental
housing are about 20 percent higher than the charges
of cooperators for similar housing. There are four
principal reasons why cooperatives can charge less
for the same housing than a rental operation.[1]

First, cooperative housing is a nonprofit
operation, where the owner-occupants derive their
benefits as the consumers of the housing. The saving
accrued is the profit reserved for the sponsor of
rental housing. Second, cooperatives do not require
allowances for vacancy and collection losses. Consequently, FHA does not require an increase in monthly
charges in cooperatives to cover such losses. In
cooperative housing with owner-occupancy, there is
greater stability of cooperatives. Third, in recognition of the stability of cooperatives and their
excellent repayment records, cooperatives are allowed
to amortize their loans under a level amortization
plan. Total payments for principal and interest
are the same each month for forty years. Finally,
there is better care of dwellings by owner occupants
in a cooperative than by tenants in rental projects,
particularly where many tenants are transients.
Therefore, the costs of maintenance and repairs are
lower.

In addition to these reported savings, it is
stated that cooperative residents are building up
an equity on the principal of the mortgage, unlike

tenants in rental housing. This particular point
is greatly misunderstood, however, and few cooperative
residents in moderate-priced co-ops ever envision
the day when their forty-year mortgage will be
completed and there will actually be an equity
realization. Resale policy in publicly administered
cooperatives does not take this into consideration,
and most publicly assisted cooperatives in this
price range do not allow the cooperative resident
to sell his unit on the private market, thereby
negating a main part of the "good investment" argument.
The principal saving realized by cooperative tenure
is the deduction allowed each cooperator for his
share of mortgage interest and real-estate taxes.
While this deduction is not sizable in publicly
financed cooperatives, such as Franklin Plaza, most
residents are aware that this tax deduction represents
a net reduction in monthly housing costs.

Respondents were asked: "Do you feel that
cooperative housing is a good investment for your
savings?" While 74 percent of the respondents
answered affirmatively, 26 percent felt that cooperative housing was not a good investment. Respondents
who answered negatively stated that the newly imposed
raise in monthly carrying charges was unfair and
financially detrimental to their personal budgets.
Yet, in spite of the increased carrying charges,
the majority of respondents indicated that they were
pleased with their investment.

FINANCING COOPERATIVE HOUSING

The proponents of a cooperative ownership policy
for low- and moderate-income families have argued,
primarily, on the basis of the social values of this
form of tenure. While the financial aspects of this
form of housing have been discussed, little has been
written on how families at this income level finance
the initial investment, or down payment, on their
apartments. The residents of Franklin Plaza were
asked if they borrowed money for the down payment
on their apartment. Of the fifty respondents interviewed, approximately half had borrowed money for

the down payment, with the remaining reporting that
they did not borrow, indicating that accrued savings
were used. Those respondents who reported that they
borrowed money for the down payment, which ranged
from approximately $1,500 for one-bedroom apartments
to $2,000 for two-bedroom apartments, were asked
the amount borrowed. Only three respondents borrowed
less than half the cost of the down payment, while
the remaining twenty-one respondents reported that
they borrowed from half to all of the down payment.

The HOPE program operated by the New York
State Division of Housing and Community Renewal, was
utilized at Franklin Plaza to provide low-interest
loans for equity investments, which were amortized
over a five-year period. The interest and principal
were to be paid on a monthly basis, along with the
monthly carrying charges. Those respondents who
borrowed money for their down payment were asked if
they were worried about borrowing for this purpose.
All but three of the twenty-four respondents reported
that they were not worried about undertaking a loan
to purchase an apartment. It is to be noted that
the three respondents who were worried were elderly
residents. The excellent financing plan available
to prospective cooperative owners through the HOPE
program seemed to diminish whatever financial burden
or risk might be expected from borrowing in the
conventional market.

THE HOME OWNERSHIP ANALOGY

Much of the confusion associated with cooperative
tenure is found in the commonly made comparison
between home ownership and ownership of a cooperative
apartment. One of the key marketing techniques used
in selling cooperative apartments, and in arguing
in favor of cooperative housing, is to list the
benefits of single-family home ownership and apply
them to cooperative ownership. It is, thus, important
to determine whether the residents of the cooperative
development being studied agree with this comparison.

As is indicated in Table 32, the majority of

TABLE 32

Franklin Plaza Respondents' Perceived
Similarities and Differences of Home
Ownership and Cooperative Ownership
(By Numerical Frequency)

Similarities and Differences	First Responses	Second Responses[a]
Similarities:		
Owning Cooperative Stock is Like Having Investment in Your Own Home	2	6
Voice in Your Own Apartment; Freedom To Do What You Want	2	3
People Are as Responsible; They Maintain Their Property	--	2
Similar; No Difference Perceived	3	5
Differences:		
Never Finish Paying for Co-op; Not Good Investment	13	13
No Freedom in a Co-op; Need Permission for Everything	3	4
Private House Is Better; Privacy and Space	6	11
Home Owners Are Better Neighbors; Nicer People	--	8
Co-ops Are Better; No Repairs or Maintenance Worries	2	7

[a]Percent with two responses, 62 percent.

Franklin respondents did not equate cooperative
ownership with single-family home ownership. Although
several respondents appreciated the investment
features of cooperative housing, most respondents
did not see the comparison.

It would appear that most respondents felt that
the analogy between home ownership and cooperative
housing was invalid from a financial and physical
point of view. The belief that investment in cooperative housing was similar to investment in a private
home was refuted by the relatively large percentage
of respondents who reported that they never would
finish paying for their apartment unit, while the
private home owner could foreseeably complete his
mortgage and own his home outright. Few residents
could envision the point in time when Franklin Plaza's
forty-year mortgage would terminate and the cooperative owners would hold full title to the development.
As in most cooperatively owned developments, few
residents foresee the day when the mortgage will be
completed and only monthly maintenance costs remain.

The fact that Franklin Plaza is a high-rise
cooperative rather than row-housing or even garden-
style housing further reduces whatever analogy made
between cooperative housing and single-family home
ownership. The traditional image of the detached,
single-family house with a private yard negated the
supposed likeness between owning a home and owning
a cooperative apartment. Although a small percentage
of respondents saw the similarity in the freedom
that both tenure forms afford their occupants, an
almost equal number felt that freedom in a cooperative
is not so great as the freedom in a private home.
Although cooperative owners are free to paint and
decorate their apartments without restraint, unlike
public housing tenants, they cannot make major
alterations in the physical structure of the apartment
unit. The privately owned home is imagined to be a
place where alterations in room layout and other
improvements are possible, which seems to be an
important point for these respondents.

Only two respondents reported that cooperative
owners share the same concern and responsibility for

their property as do private home owners. Although
the measure of responsibility in the solidarity index
indicated that group responsibility existed at
Franklin Plaza, this was not equated with the responsibility of home owners. This might merely indicate
that while Franklin Plaza residents do try to maintain the cooperative, private home owners of necessity,
must, be more directly involved in day-to-day maintenance, thus showing more responsibility toward
their residence than possible in a multiple-dwelling
development.

     Regarding the differences between the type of
person who owns his own home and the type who owns
a cooperative unit, eight respondents felt that home
owners were better neighbors and of a better class
level than the residents of cooperative housing.
The class bias associated with home ownership has
been incorporated to a relatively significant degree
into the attitudes of Franklin Plaza respondents.
Ownership is viewed as a status index by most segments
of American society, and even though cooperative
residents are "owners," it would seem that the
cooperative form of ownership is not ranked so high
in terms of status as is single-family home ownership.
The importance of self-status for families below
the national median income is an important factor
and crucial to housing policy and should be studied
in greater detail.

     As was stated earlier, home ownership is a basic
goal and value of American culture, and as Thorstein
Veblen and R.H. Tawney have pointed out, a source of
self-status in a consumption-oriented society.[2] The
arguments in favor of and against home ownership cannot
negate the importance this goal holds in the lives
of all Americans. Residents of urban slums are no
different from others in their aspirations, as many
studies have shown. In a recent survey of Harlem
residents, Joan Gordon notes that, in classifying
people who are "well-off," there is unanimity in
the belief that owning one's own home and having
a little savings in the bank constitutes an adequate
measure of the success of an individual.[3] If, indeed,
ownership is an unanimously accepted goal of Harlem
residents, it may be assumed that tenants of public

housing within these communities share this goal,
even if to a lesser extent. The question remain as
to what extent cooperative housing can provide an
alternate to single-family home ownership.

ATTITUDES REGARDING COOPERATIVE
HOUSING FOR EAST HARLEM

Cooperative owners were asked: "Would you like
to see some of the projects and buildings in the
neighborhood made into cooperatives?" Eighty percent
of the respondents indicated that they would like
to see such a policy enacted. When asked to explain
why they expressed this attitude, most respondents
saw cooperative housing as a means of improving the
neighborhood from both a physical and social stand-
point. As is shown in Table 33, the respondents
reported that cooperative housing would not only
improve the physical stock of housing but that
cooperative living would be good for the residents,
in that they would be forced to assume responsibility
for their homes and buildings. An equally large
number of responses indicated that Franklin Plaza
residents saw cooperative housing as providing
better housing for the people of the neighborhood.

These responses further indicate that cooperative
owners do perceive themselves as being members of a
unique residential community, apart from the remainder
of East Harlem. Most respondents felt that the
improved physical design of Franklin Plaza, primarily
the locked entrances and the well-designed grounds,
as well as the sense of mutual responsibility that
characterizes the cooperative, should be made available to other East Harlem residents. This concern
for providing better housing conditions for East
Harlem residents was mentioned with relatively high
frequency and indicates a general positive feeling
toward the achievements of cooperative housing.

TENURE PREFERENCE AND HOUSING ASPIRATIONS
OF PUBLIC HOUSING TENENTS

Respondents in both public housing samples were
asked a series of questions that sought to determine

TABLE 33

Franklin Plaza Residents' Attitudes
Toward Making Projects and Buildings
into Cooperatives in East Harlem
(By Numerical Frequency)

Reasons Mentioned	Number of First Responses	Number of Second Responses[a]
Yes--Neighborhood and Buildings Would Be Physically Improved	11	19
Yes--Would Be Good for People To Have Responsibility	10	4
Yes--Would Attract Better Class of People--People Concerned with Neighborhood	4	3
Yes--Would Provide Better Housing for People--End Slums	10	5
No--Should Tear Down All Tenements; Leave Projects Alone	2	1
No--Would Be Too Expensive for People Living There	8	3

[a]Percent with two responses, 78 percent.

156

their attitudes and preferences regarding tenure,
and more important, their aspirations toward cooperative housing. Two questions on housing preferences
were asked of the respondent. One question asked:
"If you could choose, would you prefer to rent or
own your own home?" As Table 34 indicates, a sizable
percentage of public housing residents prefer to
rent, although, as would be expected, the percentage
of residents who would prefer to own their own homes
was significantly larger. This was especially true

TABLE 34

Tenure and Housing Preferences of
Public Housing Tenants
(In Percent)

Preferences	Moderate-Income Sample Lexington[a]	Low-Income Sample Jefferson[a]
Tenure Preferences:		
Rent	36	40
Own	64	52
Doesn't Matter	--	8
Ideal Type of Housing Desired:		
Private Home	54	60
Different Apartment in Same Project	4	--
Apartment in Different Neighborhood	4	4
Cooperative Apartment	8	2
Remain in Present Apartment	22	26
Other	8	8
Total	100	100

[a]Fifty households sampled in each housing development.

at Lexington Houses, where home ownership would be
a possibility for families at the moderate-income
level. When asked: "What kind of place would you
like?," the respondents were encouraged by the
interviewers to state the type of housing that they
really would like and not merely prefer to have.
In examining this more hypothetical question, it is
apparent that the dream of single-family home ownership has not escaped the residents of housing projects
in East Harlem. Although a fairly large number of
residents in both developments expressed satisfaction
with their present housing, almost three out of five
respondents said they would like to own their own
homes. Only 8 percent of the Lexington sample and
2 percent of the Jefferson sample chose cooperative
housing as their choice of ideal housing type. This
finding would bear out the fact that home ownership
is an important value in the lives of public housing
residents; they are similar to residents of cooperative housing in feeling that ownership of cooperative
apartments is not equal in value to the ownership
of a private home. An equally important response
to this question was the fact that 22 percent of
Lexington respondents and 26 percent of Jefferson
respondents' first choice was to remain in their
present apartment, indicating a level of relative
satisfaction with their present living arrangement.

A measure of the aspirations of public housing
tenants was introduced by the question asking: "If
you had $2,000 or were given $2,000 tomorrow and
you had to spend the money on housing, what would
you do?" The responses to this question further
documented the two major values that public housing
tenants expressed regarding their housing. Twenty-
six percent of the Lexington sample and 38 percent
of the Jefferson sample reported that they would
use this money to improve the apartments they presently
occupied. Eight percent of Lexington respondents
would invest the $2,000 in a cooperative. Thirty-
eight percent of the Lexington respondents would
use the $2,000 to purchase their own home. Sur-
prisingly, the percentage of residents who would use
the money for a down payment on a private house was
significantly lower than the percentage of residents

who chose a private home as their first choice of
housing (see Table 35). This would seem to indicate
a realistic appraisal of the housing market in the
New York City area, where it is virtually impossible
to acquire a home with a down payment of only $2,000.
Furthermore, it would seem to indicate that a sizable
percentage of public housing residents do not have
the additional savings for a down payment, and that
the $2,000 would be better applied in the improvement
of their present apartment. Again, cooperative
housing was not shown to be a substitute for the
value placed on home ownership.

The positive attitudes toward public housing
implied in these responses was directly measured by
asking the respondents whether public housing offered
a better way of life than their previous housing.
A large portion of the critical literature on public
housing presumes that project tenants look with
nostalgia toward their former residences and consider
public housing as being inferior. The romanticism
associated with the slum is quite popular in planning
and housing literature, and, on this basis, it was
considered possible, but not likely, that a significant
number of project respondents would cite the negative
attributes of public housing.

As is shown in Table 36, the findings were far
from those that might be expected after reviewing the
literature. The majority of tenants in both projects
implied that public housing was a physical improvement
over their former residence, and, to a lesser extent,
offered an environment conducive to socialization
and child-rearing.

A possible explanation of the fact that cooperative ownership has not been chosen to a larger extent
as a preferred or idealized housing type by public
housing residents is that cooperative housing is a
relatively unusual form of housing and one that is
poorly understood, especially by people at this
socioeconomic level. To examine the effect that
lack of information has had on attitudes regarding
housing preferences, questions were asked about
knowledge of cooperative housing in general and of
Franklin Plaza in particular.

TABLE 35

Choices for Applying $2,000 to Housing
(In Percent)

Choice of Use	Moderate-Income Sample Lexington[a]	Low-Income Sample Jefferson[a]
Improve Present Apartment	26	38
Move into Another Apartment in Same Project	--	6
Buy a Cooperative Apartment at Franklin Plaza	8	4
Buy a Cooperative Apartment Outside East Harlem	4	4
Buy a Private House	38	26
Leave New York City	10	12
Rent an Apartment Outside of East Harlem	14	10
Total	100	100

[a]Fifty households sampled in each housing development.

KNOWLEDGE OF COOPERATIVE HOUSING

Public housing respondents were asked the general question: "Do you know anything about cooperative housing where you can buy your own apartment?" Sixty-eight percent of Lexington residents and 34 percent of Jefferson residents reported that they were familiar with cooperative housing. However, when asked whether the respondents knew of any cooperative housing developments in East Harlem, 86 percent of Lexington residents and 70 percent of

TABLE 36

Attitudes of Public Housing
Residents Toward Public Housing
(By Numerical Frequency)
(a)
General Response

Query	Moderate-Income Sample Lexington[a]	Low-Income Sample Jefferson[a]
Is Public Housing Better than Previous Residence?		
Yes	45	40
No	5	10

(b)

Detailed Response

Detailed Response	Moderate-Income Sample Lexington		Low-Income Sample Jefferson	
	First Response	Second Response	First Response	Second Response
	(n=45)	(n=19)	(n=45)	(n=5)
Good Maintenance, Clean, Safe	28	7	36	4
Cheap Rent, Good Value	4	3	1	1
Nice Apartments	2	3	--	--
Lots of Activities; Good for Children	2	3	2	--
Good Neighbors Here, People Help Each Other	8	3	1	--
No Difference	1	--	5	--

[a]Fifty households sampled in each housing development.

161

the Jefferson residents indicated their familiarity
with Franklin Plaza. This would seem to imply that
Franklin Plaza was at least recognized as a different
type of housing than public housing, even though it
physically resembled public housing.

To partially determine their knowledge of the
fundamental difference between cooperative tenure
and rental tenure, respondents were asked: "Did
you know that the people at Franklin Plaza own their
apartments?" The Lexington respondents were more
informed than Jefferson respondents on this financial
aspect of cooperative tenure. Seventy-two percent
of the Lexington group stated that they knew that
residents at Franklin Plaza "owned" their apartments,
while 56 percent of the Jefferson respondents stated
this. At best, these findings imply that a large
percentage of moderate-income and a smaller percentage
of low-income respondents understood rightly or
wrongly that residents of Franklin Plaza owned their
apartments and were part of a cooperatively organized
residential community.

These findings seem to indicate that a large
number of Lexington residents are reasonably knowl-
edgeable about the basic aspects of cooperative
housing, both in general and in relation to Franklin
Plaza. This is true to a lesser extent of the
Jefferson respondents. One reason for the greater
awareness at Lexington Houses is that an active sales
campaign was conducted to attract Lexington residents
to Franklin Plaza by the Franklin Plaza Corporation.
This campaign involved personal letters to tenants,
as well as the extensive use of advertising in the
project and throughout the East Harlem community.
Jefferson tenants were not actively solicited because
of their lower incomes, but the advertising campaign
was so extensive and thorough that a relatively large
proportion of respondents were probably made aware
of Franklin Plaza.

To understand further the extent to which public
housing tenants understood cooperative housing,
respondents were asked: "Do you think there are
differences when people rent their apartments like

here at Jefferson Houses/Lexington Houses than when people own their apartments like at Franklin Plaza?" Of the Lexington respondents, twenty-five reported that they thought there were differences; but an equally significant proportion, twenty respondents, reported that there were no differences, while five respondents did not answer the question. A larger number of Jefferson tenants reported that they perceived differences to exist. Only twelve Jefferson respondents saw no difference between their project and Franklin Plaza, while thirty-five respondents stated that differences exist. Three respondents at Jefferson did not answer the question.

Respondents were asked to elaborate on this statement, as is recorded in Table 37. The major differences thought to exist related to the belief that when people own their apartment, they take better care of the property. The cleanliness of Franklin Plaza was taken to be a major difference between cooperative housing and rental housing. Also reported in less significant detail was the belief that residents of a cooperative have more freedom to express their opinions in the operation of the development. Safety was a more important factor for Jefferson respondents than for Lexington respondents, reflecting, in part, the low degree of solidarity and mutual trust that was found to exist in this low-income project.

Powerful in the literature on urban redevelopment is the belief that the introduction of housing alternatives into a community previously without such alternatives will lead to increased level of aspiration and achievement directions for its residents. Franklin Plaza was the first moderate-income cooperative to be built in East Harlem and, as such, should generate its own magnetism, thereby developing and channeling the housing aspirations of residents of the area toward cooperative ownership. This is especially true for families who could not compete in the conventional private home market in New York City, since cooperative housing affords the possibility of a form of ownership for families whose income level would normally limit their choice of housing.

TABLE 37

Perceived Differences Between
Franklin Plaza and Public Housing
(By Numerical Frequency)

Differences	Moderate-Income Sample Lexington		Low-Income Sample Jefferson	
	First Response	Second Response	First Response	Second Response
Cooperative Owners Take Better Care of Their Property; More Responsible	10	1	5	--
Able To Have Voice in Making Decisions	4	1	3	--
Apartments Are Nicer	1	1	1	--
Safer in Cooperative, More Guards, Locked Doors	1	1	6	--
Wealthier People Live in Cooperatives	4	2	3	--
Only Difference Is Expense	9	1	11	--
No Difference-- Same as a Project	11	2	11	--

In addition to providing an alternative to
renting in public housing, it was presumed by the
sponsors of Franklin Plaza that a cooperative would
serve to provide housing for moderate-income families
who were attached to the East Harlem neighborhood
but were unable to find suitable housing. The
sentiments and loyalty to this particular New York

City neighborhood were presumed to be strong, and
it was expected that housing project tenants would
cite neighborhood values as a reason for wanting
to live in Franklin Plaza, if it were possible.
This expectation was further encouraged by the literature on public housing, which claims that public
housing tenants are not pleased with their form of
housing and would respond strongly to the opportunity
to own their own apartments within a neighborhood
familiar to them.

To measure the impact of Franklin Plaza on the
housing aspirations of public housing tenants,
respondents were asked: "If you could choose, would
you like to live in Franklin Plaza?" Of the Lexington
residents, 22 percent indicated that they would,
while 64 percent reported that they would not like
to live in the cooperative (see Table 38). A higher
number of Jefferson residents, 46 percent, indicated
that they would like to live there, while 52 percent
answered negatively. Two respondents at Lexington
and one at Jefferson were undecided and gave no
answer. Those respondents who indicated that they
would not like to live there were asked to indicate
their reason for this decision. Respondents who
answered negatively reported that Franklin Plaza was
too expensive or not worth the cost of occupancy.

A significant number of Lexington residents
indicated that they would rather buy their own home,
since Franklin Plaza was not worth the money because
of its location in East Harlem. Respondents, also,
reported that they saw no difference between Franklin
Plaza and their public housing projects. A significant
number of Jefferson residents reported that they
would prefer to remain in the project, implying
either that Franklin Plaza was not very much of an
improvement over their present housing or that the
harsh reality of their current and projected income
level will exclude them from entertaining the notion
of moving from the low-income project.

Those residents who indicated that they would
like to live in Franklin Plaza were asked if they
had ever thought of moving into Franklin Plaza.

TABLE 38

Reasons For Not Wanting to
Live in Franklin Plaza
(By Numerical Frequency)

Reasons Reported	Moderate-Income Sample Lexington	Low-Income Sample Jefferson
Too Expensive	8	8
No Money for the Down Payment	1	1
Prefer To Buy Own Home--Not Worth Money in East Harlem	11	2
Prefer To Remain in Project	6	13
Rather Leave East Harlem	3	--
No Different than Project	3	2

Of the eleven respondents in Lexington Houses who
reported that they would like to live in the cooperative, nine reported that they had thought of moving
there. Of the twenty-three respondents at Jefferson
who mentioned that they would like to live in Franklin
Plaza, eight had thought of moving there. Obviously
their plans ended at the thought stage, and these
respondents were asked: "Why haven't you move there?"
Five of the respondents in each project reported
that Franklin Plaza was too expensive, while the
remainder stated that they did not have the money
for the down payment required to purchase an apartment.
These findings indicate that almost one out of five
of the respondents reported that they had thought
of purchasing a cooperative apartment but that
Franklin Plaza was considered to be too expensive.
The monthly carrying charges in the cooperative were
slightly higher than the rents charged at Lexington

Houses, but the $2,000 down payment for a two-bedroom
apartment was a large sum of money and a major
expense for most budgets. Although the larger
expense per se might explain the failure of these
respondents to move into the cooperative, it might
also be possible that while these residents thought
of moving to Franklin Plaza, they felt that its
expense was not worthwhile. Looking back to Table
35, only 8 percent, or four Lexington respondents,
indicated that they would use the hypothetical $2,000
to purchase an apartment at Franklin. Only 4 percent,
or two of the Jefferson respondents, reported that
they would use this money, if made available, to
move to Franklin Plaza.

In spite of the indication that the majority
of the respondents were aware of Franklin Plaza's
existence and its cooperative form of tenure, it
might be that project residents were under the
impression that Franklin Plaza was for wealthier
families or that they would not be welcome if they
decided to move there. Although only a few respondents
indicated that they perceived this to be true, it
was possible that they would desire to own a cooperative apartment if their present housing project was
converted to a cooperative. This is especially
relevant to the large number of residents who reported
that they were pleased with their present housing
and saw no reason to move into Franklin Plaza. To
measure the extent to which cooperative tenure would
be accepted by public housing tenants if such policy
was carried out, the respondents were asked: "Would
you like to be able to own the apartment you are now
living in if this project was made a cooperative?"
One-half of the Lexington respondents reported that
they would, as did 48 percent of the Jefferson
respondents. This seems to show that project residents were at least open to the idea of a change in
tenure policy for their project. However, when
asked: "If this project was made a cooperative,
would you be willing to borrow money to buy an
apartment here?" the proportion decreased significantly. Only 28 percent of the Lexington residents
and 30 percent of the Jefferson residents would be
willing to borrow money to purchase their apartment,

if a cooperative tenure policy was adopted. Thus,
the initial willingness was reported, apart from
the financial reality required to own a cooperative
apartment.

SUMMARY

     Several salient points regarding housing policy
and housing aspirations can be drawn from the investigation of the attitudes of the two groups of public
housing tenants. Contrary to the critical literature
on public housing, the moderate-income public housing
group and, to a lesser extent, the low-income group
expressed positive attitudes toward their present
form of housing. This finding was especially significant for the low-income project respondents, in
that the analysis of measures of the overall social
environment in that project indicated that this
project was the least desirable of the three developments studied. In spite of definite shortcomings
in public housing, such as insufficient protection
for residents from negative elements in the East
Harlem community, the residents indicated that public
housing offered a better way of life, both environ-
mentally and socially, than they could hope to obtain
on the private market.

     The residents of Franklin Plaza were equally
positive in their attitudes toward cooperative
housing. It is significant that a large percentage
of those interviewed at Franklin Plaza viewed cooperative housing as not only a means of improving housing
in East Harlem but indicated that, if cooperative
tenure was adapted to existing projects and apartment
houses, East Harlem residents would be inculcated
with some of the values of cooperative living,
especially responsibility toward the residential
environment. Cooperative tenure was viewed not as
a goal in itself but, mainly, as means to other ends.
Specifically, cooperative tenure was seen as a means
of improving living conditions rather than as a means
of achieving emotional, financial or social goals.

     The aspiration toward home ownership is a

relatively important factor in the lives of both
public housing groups surveyed, although it is
significant in terms of the literature on the subject
that almost one-half of those interviewed were
indifferent to ownership. Considering the positive
attitudes expressed toward public housing, it would
be difficult to ignore this indifference, just as
it would be difficult to ignore the aspirations of
residents toward home ownership.

The question arises as to whether cooperative
ownership can meet the aspirations of those public
housing residents who have indicated their preference
for ownership rather than renting. More important
is the degree to which cooperative tenure represents
a means of translating ownership aspirations into
an action-oriented goal, toward which people are
willing to undertake the financial commitment necessary
to achieve this goal. A sizable number of respondents
in both housing projects indicated that they would
like to live in Franklin Plaza if they had the choice.
A smaller but significant number of these respondents
reported that they had given serious thought of
moving into the cooperative, but were either unable
or unwilling to assume the added costs of cooperative
ownership. This would seem to imply that cooperative
ownership was viewed as an alternative to the more
desirable aspiration of private home ownership for
at least a measurable percentage of tenants in public
housing. However, ownership of a cooperative apartment, virtually identical to the one they occupied,
and in the same neighborhood, was not a sufficient
goal to direct latent or real ownership aspirations
toward cooperative ownership at Franklin Plaza. In
addition to these factors and the added cost of
living at Franklin Plaza, the positive attitudes
expressed toward public housing would seem to further
reduce the force necessary to attract residents of
public rental housing to cooperatively owned housing.
The very small number of former public housing tenants
would seem to further document this observation.

The idea of moving from public housing to the
Franklin Plaza cooperative was expressed by similar
numbers of respondents in both projects, but an even

larger number of residents indicated that they saw
no reason to move from their projects. This was
further evidenced by the fact that almost 30 percent
of the respondents from both the Lexington and the
Jefferson projects indicated that they would be
willing to borrow money to remain in their project
if it were converted to cooperative ownership. While
these data indicate that cooperative tenure in place
of rental tenure is not a unanimous choice of public
housing residents, it does seem that cooperative
tenure would be accepted by a fairly large number
of the respondents interviewed if they did not have
to move from their public housing project. This
finding must be critically analyzed for future policy
decisions, in that it would seem that cooperative
tenure is not viewed as an end in itself but rather,
for these respondents, as a means of attaining basic
physical improvements in their existing form of
housing. A more cynical interpretation of this
finding might be that public housing residents have
been so intimidated by the possibility of eviction
for a wide variety of reasons that they will emphati-
cally express their willingness to do anything that
ensures their continued occupancy.

NOTES

1. David L. Krooth, "How Cooperative Housing
Can Help Urban Renewal," in Jerome Liblit, ed.,
op. cit., pp. 102-3.

2. Ownership is an index of status in many
studies. Talcott Parsons notes the function of
accumulated goods, including property, in his article
"An Analytical Approach to the Theory of Social
Stratification," American Journal of Sociology,
V (May, 1940), 481-82.

3. Joan Gordon, "The Poor of Harlem: Social
Functioning in the Underclass" (New York: Office
of the Major; Interdepartmental Neighborhood Service
Center, 1965), p. 33. Similar findings were reported
in Theodore Caplow, "Home Ownership and Location
Preferences in a Minnesota Sample," American Sociological Review, XIII (December, 1948), 725-30.

9

The purpose of this study was to examine the relationship of tenure to a set of social phenomena, contrasting cooperative tenure with rental tenure in public housing. The method of inquiry employed also made possible an examination of a full range of variables, other than tenure, which are related to the social functioning of a residential development. In this fashion, a perspective was provided of the various factors that are related to the evaluation of selected social phenomena, as well as to the interdependence of these factors with the tenure variable.

The general proposition on which the hypotheses of this study were formulated was that cooperative tenure is related to higher levels of neighborly interaction, community solidarity, housing attitudes, pride in residence and participation in community activities, than would be found with rental tenure. Hypotheses were formulated into testable statements of relationship between these dependent variables and the independent variable, tenure. The hypotheses were tested by the use of data obtained from field interviews. The sample population consisted of two moderate-income populations, one group with coopera- tive tenure and the other with rental tenure. A third group consisted of residents of a low-income public housing rental project. This latter group provided a means for evaluating the effect of

171

socioeconomic variables, other than tenure, on the
hypotheses tested.

There were no statistically significant differences between the two moderate-income groups in the
scores achieved in the specific measures of neighborly interaction, community solidarity or community
participation, although the Franklin Plaza respondents
scored slightly higher in these measures than did
the comparative Lexington group. Low-income residents
achieved significantly lower scores than did the
moderate-income groups in all of the measures used.
The significance found was useful in establishing
a perspective from which to analyze the results of
this study in terms of their implications for housing
policy.

Many questions remain unanswered with regard to
the implications of cooperative tenure as a possible
alternative to existing rental policy in public
housing. It is not indicated here that cooperative
housing has significant social advantages over public
rental housing when the populations are similar as
to socioeconomic factors. The strongest evidence in
support of the greater social effects of cooperative
tenure was the greater sense of responsibility toward
the maintenance of common property and the apparent
pride derived from residency in Franklin Plaza.
However, it must be questioned whether the existence
of physical improvements at Franklin Plaza, such as
the architecturally designed grounds and safety precautions, were significant factors leading to a
greater sense of pride and responsibility. Franklin
Plaza was also newer than the Lexington Houses, and
the combination of these factors might very well be
related to the higher levels of pride and responsibility reported by Franklin Plaza respondents. This
question becomes especially relevant in that the
reason given for favoring cooperative tenure centered
upon the physical improvements that Franklin Plaza
offered and not the hypothesized social effects.

The question, also, must be raised as to whether
cooperative owners have rationalized their pride and
positive feelings. Although the data provide no

accurate vertification, it is possible that cooperative owners have persuaded themselves that they are
supposed to a feel a stronger responsibility toward
physical maintenance than they would if they were
renting apartments, or, perhaps, they have been so
influenced by the cooperative education programs
that they are merely reiterating the assumptions
made regarding the benefits of cooperative tenure.
Although the findings regarding pride and responsibility are significant, these questions must at
least be considered in interpreting the dimensions
of these relationships.*

From a more optimistic perspective, these same
findings might also be indicators of the existence
of a viable social community, in which shared
responsibility and the indirect expression of pride
in residence is a result of cooperative tenure. It
might very well be that the measures used to qualify
certain aspects of community solidarity, neighborly
interaction and, to a lesser extent, participation
in community affairs, were not as effective as had
been expected. One of the basic parameters used to
determine the existence of community solidarity is
consensus on norms affecting the behavior of members
of a group. The transmission of norms is a much
less important aspect of community functioning than
the actual acceptance of these norms into the value
structure of the members of that community. The
sharing of responsibility toward the physical maintenance of property held in common is considered by
many to be a major norm or value to be instilled in
the members of a residential community. The case
can be made that consequences on this aspect of communal living is the foundation from which individual
and community development may emanate, factors such
as group identification, the desire to participate
in community life and active socialization and

---

*The issue of rationalization of the benefits
of ownership is best presented in a case against
home ownership in John P. Dean, Home Ownership: Is
It Sound? (New York: Harper and Brothers, 1945).

interaction may very well be developing within the
Franklin Plaza Cooperative, and the finding regarding
shared responsibility may be the initial indicator
of such development.

The findings of this study seem to indicate
that although socioeconomic status and not tenure
are associated with most social phenomena, the tenure
variable does seem to be related to the acceptance
or perception of shared responsibility. The extent
to which this finding is an indicator of more fundamental attributes of what has been termed "community"
deserves further inquiry in housing research.

In analyzing the attitudes of both cooperative
owners and public housing tenants, positive feelings
toward the housing environment were more common to
all groups than were negative feelings. The desire
for cleanliness and adequate apartments was found in
all groups. The emphasis placed on safety by public
housing residents is especially significant, for it
influenced strongly the perception of what cooperative
tenure at Franklin Plaza could offer. It would be
interesting to observe if the mere addition of locked
entrances and an increase in the number of guards in
public housing projects would result in an even more
positive evaluation of public housing by its residents, and more important, an equal sense of pride
and responsibility.

A more basic question arises out of the evaluation of housing attitudes and aspirations. While
home ownership was a common enough goal among a
large percentage of public housing tenants, a sub-
stantial number of tenants were indifferent to ownership. More important for this study was the indifference expressed toward cooperative ownership in
Franklin Plaza. Although several respondents in
both moderate- and low-income projects reported that
they had thought about moving from public housing
into the cooperative, they felt that cooperative
ownership in a development that was not substantially
different from their present residence, as well as
being in the same unsatisfactory neighborhood, was
not worth the added expense. The positive attitudes

regarding public housing also entered into the
rationale for not choosing to live in Franklin Plaza.
These findings would seem to imply that cooperative
ownership at Franklin Plaza is not a significant
aspirational goal for public housing residents in
these two East Harlem projects. Rather, public
housing is accepted by its residents with varying
degrees of enthusiasm, depending upon sociocultural
and economic levels, as providing a healthy and
positive housing environment.

The point must also be raised regarding the
administrative and financial aspects of the Franklin
Plaza cooperative and most publicly subsidized
cooperatives. The hypotheses that this study sought
to test were formulated on the basis of what was
largely conceptual, or theoretical, literature,
rather than a literature based on operational realities. It can be argued with considerable force that
Franklin Plaza was not a true cooperative. This
case might be made on the grounds that major decisions
regarding financing and monthly costs were made not
by the members of the cooperative but by the public
agency administering the mortgage. Also, the fact
that the initial investment, or downpayment, was not
really a profit-oriented investment but a payment
for an apartment in a constrained housing market
might very well have resulted in the findings of
this study being far from what had been hypothesized.
Existing public policy does not permit the cooperative
resident to sell his apartment unit at a profit nor
is he given interest on his initial investment.
Even more basic is the fact that this investment is
not adjusted for inflation, and the cooperator is
not allowed to claim a share of the equity accumulated
by the corporation when he sells his apartment after
several years of residence in the cooperative. Thus,
an investment of $2,000 made in 1962 is not adjusted
in 1971 to account for inflation or property appreciation but, instead, remains fixed at the initial
rate and return at that price level. The reality
of this fact is that the cooperator loses money when
viewed strictly in terms of investment criteria.

The dilemma policy makers concerned with housing

must face is whether to allow residents of publicly subsidized cooperatives to make a profit when they sell their apartments or keep the equity investment as low as possible so as to allow families with marginal incomes and limited savings to purchase apartments. The answer to such a dilemma, in part, rests on the proof that cooperative tenure is related to social benefits that are not possible in rental housing. The fact that this study did not provide many positive findings to support the argument in favor of cooperative tenure can potentially be explained in light of the administrative and financial nature of Franklin Plaza, which could not possibly foster the hypothesized social effects or by the fact that socioeconomic status and not tenure is related to social behavior.

In view of the current emphasis placed on cooperative tenure in housing policy directed toward low- and moderate-income families, there exists a great need to investigate further the dimensions of cooperative housing. Investigation into the internal organization of cooperative housing and the processes developed for residents to participate in management decisions is especially vital in light of the needs of Black and Puerto Rican communities for managerial expertise. The economic consequences of investment in cooperative housing by marginal-income families should also be investigated, especially with regard to the concepts of opportunity-loss and opportunity-gain. The consequences of encouraging moderate-income families to invest and remain in a predominantly low-income community should receive attention, in addition to the examination of the meaning and implications of heterogeneity, social mobility and the metropolitan labor market. More work in the study of public housing's social aspects is needed, since the body of literature on the subject has been more critical than constructive. Perhaps, the most pressing research needs in this aspect of housing policy would be theoretical and empirical investigations into the very nature of ownership as goal and value and its implications for contemporary and projected American society.

The findings of this study will lead hopefully
to continued research on the needs and realities of
the residents of the vertical residential developments
of our urban areas. Over the past few years, housing
policy has incorporated social objectives, as well
as economic and shelter objectives, in attempting to
orient programs toward consumer needs, as well as to
market realities. This emphasis must continue, and
its translation should be effectuated throughout
the public and private institutions involved in the
delivery of housing services. In no way should the
findings presented in this study deter those concerned
with achieving broader social objectives through
housing policy, whether it be the cooperative housing
movement or the federal programs designed to provide
choice in tenure and residence. Any future proposals
to alter the tenure structure of public housing on
the basis of social objectives should bear the
findings of this study in mind in assessing the costs
and benefits involved for the residents. The impli-
cation of this study would suggest that while there
are some social effects related specifically to
cooperative tenure, these same effects might easily
be realized by a reexamination of the policies and
programs of public rental housing.

APPENDIX

APPENDIX

THE FIELD SURVEY INSTRUMENT

Job #5057

  S Study

CONFIDENTIAL

Family and Community Teams   Development (circle)

                                              1 Franklin Plaza

                                              2 Lexington Houses

                                              3 Jefferson Houses

Name _____

Address _____

Apartment Number _____

Phone Number _____

Job #5057

Field Survey Instrument

S STUDY

C O N F I D E N T I A L

Date of Interview:

_____

Time Started: ____AM ____PM

Time Finished: ____AM ____PM

Interviewer:

_____

PART I

INTERVIEWER: Read outloud all questions and responses printed in CAPITALS on right of double line. Note and understand instructions on left.

Instructions to Interviewer	Questions and Responses

Lexington and Jefferson Houses are the projects. Franklin Plaza is the co-op. Use the formal name of project or co-op whenever noted.

1. HOW LONG HAVE YOU LIVED IN (FRANKLIN PLAZA/LEXINGTON HOUSES/JEFFERSON HOUSES)?   (years) _____
                    Less than 1 year.....   0

2. HOW LONG HAVE YOU LIVED IN THIS APARTMENT?   (years) _____
                    Less than 1 year.....   0

3. WHEN YOU MOVED INTO (FRANKLIN PLAZA/ LEXINGTON HOUSES/JEFFERSON HOUSES), HOW LONG DID YOU PLAN ON STAYING?
                    Less than 1 year.....   0
                    1 - 3 years.........   1
                    4 - 6 years.........   2
                    7 - 10 years........   3
                    Over 19 years.......   4
                    Forever.............   5
                    No definite plans....   6
                    Other (specify) _____

                    _____

                    _____

4. HOW LONG HAVE YOU LIVED IN EAST HARLEM?
                    (years) _____
                    Less than 1 year.....   0

Specify _East_ Harlem.
East Harlem is that
area between E. 96th
and E. 130th Streets,
from Park Avenue to
the East River.

If New York City
ask part of city.

5a. DID YOU LIVE IN EAST HARLEM BEFORE
     MOVING TO (FRANKLIN PLAZA/LEXINGTON
     HOUSES/JEFFERSON HOUSES)?

               Yes (go to 6)... 1
               No (ask b)...... 2

  b. WHERE DID YOU LIVE BEFORE MOVING HERE?

_____

_____

_____

_____

6. WHAT KIND OF HOUSING DID YOU LIVE IN
    BEFORE MOVING HERE?

               Housing project......   1
               Apartment house......   2
               Private house........   3
               Cooperative..........   4
               Other (specify)......   5

"Neighborhood"
means East Harlem.

7. DO YOU THINK THAT YOUR NEIGHBORHOOD
    HAS IMPROVED, REMAINED THE SAME, OR
    HAS GOTTEN WORSE SINCE YOU FIRST MOVED
    IN?

               Improved.............   3
               About the same.......   2
               Worse................   1

Column A: Record everyone in household even if not related. List relationship to head like son, daughter, mother-in-law.

Include: member in hospital but not institutions.

Do not include: member in armed forces.

Column B: Age at last birthday.

Column C: Record highest year completed. Write in: trade, correspondence, adult education, on-the-job training.

Column D: "Parochial" includes private school.

8. NOW I WOULD LIKE TO ASK YOU SOME QUESTIONS ABOUT YOUR FAMILY...THOSE THAT LIVE HERE IN THIS APARTMENT WITH YOU.

   a. FIRST, MAY I ASK WHO LIVES HERE? I DON'T NEED NAMES. (Enter responses under Column A below. Put X beside respondent.)

   b. HOW OLD ARE THEY? LET'S START WITH YOU. (Enter responses under Column B below.)

   c. HOW FAR DID YOU GO IN SCHOOL? THE OTHERS? (Enter responses under Column C below.)

   d. (Ask only if children in school.) DOES YOUR (SON, DAUGHTER) GO TO PUBLIC OR PAROCHIAL SCHOOL?

A. Household members	B. Age in years	C. Highest grade completed	D. Pub-lic	Pri-vate
Husband				
Wife				
Children				
Other relatives or nonrelatives				

   e. (Ask only of those without husband/wife.) ARE YOU WIDOWED, SEPARATED, DIVORCED, OR SINGLE?

      Widowed..... 2   Divorced...... 4

      Separated... 3   Single 5

Ask employment infor-
mation for both husband
and wife if both are
living in household.

9a. ARE YOU AND YOUR (HUSBAND, WIFE)
EMPLOYED?

Wife........ Yes....... 1
.... No (ask b) 2

Husband..... Yes....... 1
.... No (ask b) 2

b. ARE YOU (IS HE) ......

	Wife	Husband
UNEMPLOYED	5	5
DISABLED	6	6
RETIRED	7	7
HOUSEWIFE	8	

OTHER (specify below)

If "housewife"
do not ask Q10.

If "other" write in
complete explanation.

Wife _____

Husband _____

For retired, disabled,
unemployed, be sure to
get occupation (job worked
at most of life).

10. WHAT IS (WAS) YOUR (YOUR HUSBAND'S)
MAJOR OCCUPATION?

Wife _____
            (occupation)

_____

Record major
occupation of both
respondents. State
in detail, including
name of job.

Husband _____
              (occupation)

_____

11. WHEN YOU WERE LOOKING FOR APARTMENTS WAS (FRANKLIN PLAZA/LEXINGTON HOUSES/JEFFERSON HOUSES) YOUR FIRST CHOICE?

Yes.......... 1

No.......... 2

12. WHOSE IDEA WAS IT TO MOVE TO (FRANKLIN PLAZA/ LEXINGTON HOUSES/JEFFERSON HOUSES)?

Husband.............. 1

Wife................ 2

Children............ 3

Relative............ 4

Friend.............. 5

Social agency........ 6

Other (specify)...... 7

_____

_____

13a. DO YOU LIKE YOUR APARTMENT?

Very much (skip to 14).. 1

Somewhat (skip to 14)... 2

Dislike (ask b)........ 3

Other _____ 4

b. IS IT BECAUSE IT IS TOO SMALL?

Yes (ask c)............ 1

No (skip to 14)........ 2

Ask only if major dislike seems to be the small size of apartment.

c. WOULD YOU LIKE TO HAVE A LARGER APARTMENT HERE IF SUCH WAS AVAILABLE?

Yes.................... 1

No.................... 2

14. DO YOU FEEL PROUD WHEN YOU TELL OTHERS THAT YOU LIVE AT (FRANKLIN PLAZA/LEXINGTON HOUSES/JEFFERSON HOUSES)?

Yes.................. 1

No................... 2

15a. HAVE YOU EVER TRIED TO GET YOUR FRIENDS TO MOVE IN HERE?

Yes.................. 1

No................... 2

b. HAVE YOU EVER TRIED TO GET YOUR RELATIVES TO MOVE IN HERE?

Yes.................. 1

No................... 2

16. DO YOU THINK THAT THE PEOPLE HERE TRY HARD TO SEE THAT THE BUILDING IS KEPT CLEAN AND NEAT?

Yes.................. 1

No................... 2

Some do, some don't... 3

17. IF YOU NOTICED CHILDREN MARKING UP THE LOBBY OF THIS BUILDING, WHAT WOULD YOU DO?

"Stop them immediately" can mean any action taken on the spot when respondent sees children marking up lobby.

Stop them immediately......... 1

Call their parents........... 2

Call the manager............. 3

Call a neighbor.............. 4

Mind my own business
(do nothing)........... 5

Don't care................... 6

Other (specify)..............; 7

_____

Read aloud each age
group and have R.
answer for each age
group.

18. I WOULD LIKE TO KNOW YOUR OPINION ON WHETHER YOU
THINK THE (PROJECT/CO-OP) HELPS PEOPLE HERE TO
GET ALONG WITH EACH OTHER.

		Yes	No
a.	HOW ABOUT.......YOUNG CHILDREN......	1	2
b.	HOW ABOUT.......TEENAGERS...........	1	2
c.	HOW ABOUT.......PARENTS.............	1	2
d.	HOW ABOUT.......THE OLDER PEOPLE....	1	2

19a. DO YOU EVER GO TO ACTIVITIES IN THE COMMUNITY
CENTER HERE IN THE (PROJECT/CO-OP)?

Yes......... 1

No.......... 2

Ask b if respondent
has children under
19 years old.

b. DO YOUR CHILDREN GO TO THE ACTIVITIES IN THE
(PROJECT/CO-OP) FOR THEM?

Yes......... 1

No.......... 2

Explain, if necessary
that "associate with"
can mean...to be
friends, to visit
with, etc.

20. DO YOU FEEL MORE COMFORTABLE TO ASSOCIATE WITH
PEOPLE THAT LIVE IN THE (PROJECT/CO-OP) OR DO
YOU FEEL MORE COMFORTABLE TO ASSOCIATE WITH
PEOPLE FROM THE NEIGHBORHOOD?

Only in project/co-op... 1

Some of each; both...... 2

Neighborhood............ 3

Doesn't matter.......... 4

Other _____ 5

"Here"...in the
project/co-op

21a. DO YOU THINK THAT THE PEOPLE WHO LIVE IN THE
NEIGHBORHOOD ARE DIFFERENT FROM THE PEOPLE WHO
LIVE HERE?

Yes........ 1

No......... 2

b. WHY WOULD YOU SAY THAT?

Probe _____

Probe _____

Probe

189

22a. WOULD YOU SAY THAT (FRANKLIN PLAZA/LEXINGTON HOUSES/JEFFERSON HOUSES) IS AN <u>EXCELLENT</u>, <u>GOOD</u> OR <u>BAD</u> PLACE TO LIVE IN?

Excellent............. 1
Good.................. 2
So-so; fair........... 3
Bad................... 4
Very bad.............. 5
Other................. 6

b. WHY WOULD YOU SAY THAT?

<u>Probe</u> _____

<u>Probe</u> _____

<u>Probe</u> _____

_____

_____

_____

23a. WOULD YOU SAY THAT IT IS DIFFICULT OR EASY TO MAKE FRIENDS IN THIS BUILDING?

Very easy............. 5
Easy.................. 4
So-so................. 3
Difficult............. 2
Very difficult........ 1

Other buildings here in the project/co-op.

b. WOULD YOU SAY THAT IT IS DIFFICULT OR EASY TO MAKE FRIENDS WITH PEOPLE IN OTHER BUILDINGS?

Very easy............. 5
Easy.................. 4
So-so................. 3
Difficult............. 2
Very difficult........ 1

24. ABOUT HOW MANY OF THE PEOPLE IN YOUR (PROJECT/CO-OP) DO YOU SAY "HELLO" OR "GOOD MORNING" TO WHEN YOU MEET DOWNSTAIRS?

$$\text{Six or more............ 2}$$
$$\text{Five or less........... 1}$$

25. DO YOU HAVE SOMEONE YOU CONSIDER A BEST FRIEND WHO LIVES HERE IN THE (PROJECT/CO-OP)?

$$\text{Yes.................... 1}$$
$$\text{No..................... 2}$$

26. ABOUT HOW MANY OF THE PEOPLE WHO LIVE HERE WOULD YOU RECOGNIZE BY SIGHT IF YOU SEE THEM IN A LARGE CROWD?

$$\text{None................... 0}$$
$$\text{Few.................... 1}$$
$$\text{Many................... 2}$$
$$\text{Most................... 3}$$

27. I'M NOW GOING TO READ YOU A STATEMENT. IF YOU THINK IT IS A TRUE STATE-MENT, SAY TRUE. IF YOU THINK IT IS A FALSE STATEMENT, SAY FALSE.

	True	False
a. REAL FRIENDS ARE HARD TO FIND IN THIS (PROJECT/CO-OP).....................................	1	2
b. FAMILIES IN THIS (PROJECT/CO-OP) KEEP THEIR CHILDREN UNDER CONTROL............................	1	2
c. PEOPLE WON'T WORK TOGETHER TO GET THINGS DONE IN THIS (PROJECT/CO-OP)...........................	1	2
d. PEOPLE HERE ARE UNCONCERNED ABOUT WHAT THEIR CHILDREN DO SO LONG AS THEY KEEP OUT OF TROUBLE....	1	2
e. MOST PEOPLE GET THEIR FAMILIES TO SUNDAY SCHOOL OR CHURCH ON SUNDAY................................	1	2
f. NOBODY SEEMS TO CARE MUCH HOW THE (PROJECT/CO-OP) LOOKS..	1	2
g. A LOT OF PEOPLE HERE THINK THEY ARE TOO GOOD FOR YOU...	1	2
h. THE PEOPLE AS A WHOLE MIND THEIR OWN BUSINESS......	1	2
i. IF THEIR CHILDREN KEEP OUT OF THE WAY, PARENTS ARE SATISFIED TO LET THEM DO WHATEVER THEY WANT TO DO..	1	2

28. NOW I'D LIKE TO ASK SOME QUESTIONS ABOUT YOUR NEIGHBORS. THOSE WHO LIVE IN YOUR BUILDING.....

	Yes	No
Yes can include often; once in a while; sometimes occasionally.		
a. DO YOU AND YOUR NEIGHBORS TALK ABOUT WHERE THE BEST PLACES ARE TO SHOP?	1	2
b. DO YOU AND YOUR NEIGHBORS EVER TALK ABOUT HOW TO RAISE CHILDREN?	1	2
c. DO YOU AND YOUR NEIGHBORS TALK ABOUT PROBLEMS IN THE BUILDING?	1	2
d. DO YOU EVER MIND EACH OTHER'S CHILD?	1	2
e. IN THE LAST COUPLE OF WEEKS HAVE YOU AND YOUR NEIGHBORS IN THE BUILDING EVER LOANED ONE ANOTHER A DOLLAR OR SO?	1	2
f. DO YOU AND YOUR NEIGHBORS EVER PLAY CARDS OR WATCH TELEVISION TOGETHER?	1	2
g. DO YOU AND YOUR NEIGHBORS EVER HAVE A DRINK TOGETHER?	1	2

If respondent has no children, ask if he or she ever watches a neighbor's child.

29. IF SOMEONE IN THIS BUILDING KEPT ON HAVING NOISY PARTIES THAT DISTURBED YOU, WHAT WOULD YOU DO?

Probe _____

Probe _____

Probe _____

30. WHAT DO YOU THINK ABOUT THIS NEIGHBORHOOD AS A PLACE TO LIVE?

    Like it a lot........... 3
    It's ok................. 2
    Don't like it at all..... 1

31. DO YOU THINK THAT THE PEOPLE WHO LIVE HERE IN (FRANKLIN PLAZA/LEXINGTON HOUSES/JEFFERSON HOUSES) ARE HARDER WORKING PEOPLE THAN THOSE WHO LIVE OUTSIDE THE (PROJECT/CO-OP) IN THE NEIGHBORHOOD?

    Yes..................... 1
    No...................... 2
    About the same 3

32. IN THE PAST YEAR DID YOU DO ANY OF THE FOLLOWING:

	Yes	No
a. CONTRIBUTE MONEY TO A CHURCH.....................	1	2
b. CONTRIBUTE MONEY FOR OTHER CHARITIES LIKE THE MARCH OF DIMES, THE RED CROSS, ETC...............	1	2
c. TAKE PART IN ANY COMMITTEE IN THE (RPOJECT/CO-OP) RESPONSIBLE FOR IMPROVING CONDITIONS HERE.........	1	2
d. TAKE PART IN ANY COMMITTEE OR CLUB WORKING TO IMPROVE CONDITIONS IN THE NEIGHBORHOOD............	1	2
e. LEAD ANY GROUP OR COMMITTEE AS AN OFFICER.........	1	2
f. CONTRIBUTE MONEY TO ONE OF THE POVERTY PROGRAMS OR ANY OTHER PROGRAMS TRYING TO IMPROVE LIFE IN THE NEIGHBORHOOD..............................	1	2
g. TRY TO LEARN ABOUT PROBLEMS AND ISSUES IN THE NEIGHBORHOOD...................................	1	2
h. DISCUSS THESE PROBLEMS FREQUENTLY WITH MORE THAN ONE PERSON....................................	1	2
i. TRY TO PERSUADE YOUR NEIGHBORS TO LEARN ABOUT PROBLEMS IN THE NEIGHBORHOOD AND TO DO SOME- ING ABOUT THEM....................................	1	2
j. GET ADVICE FROM OTHERS ABOUT SOME OF THESE PROBLEMS..	1	2
k. SPEAK TO KEY LEADERS IN THE PROJECT/CO-OP ABOUT PROBLEMS.....................................	1	2
l. VISIT COMMUNITY ORGANIZATIONS AND TENANTS COUNCILS LIKE MEND OR METRO NORTH TO LEARN OF ISSUES IN THE NEIGHBORHOOD.................................	1	2
m. WRITE LETTERS OR HOLD MEETINGS IN YOUR HOUSE ABOUT CONDITIONS IN THE NEIGHBORHOOD..............	1	2

33. DO YOU THINK THAT YOU CAN DO SOMETHING ABOUT GETTING BETTER SERVICES SUCH AS IMPROVED SCHOOLS AND PARKS FOR EAST HARLEM?

Yes................. 1

No................. 2

34. AS A RESIDENT OF THE (PROJECT/CO-OP) DO YOU FEEL YOU SHOULD TRY TO IMPROVE EAST HARLEM?

Yes................. 1

No................. 2

Include PTA, school
groups, church groups
in the neighborhood,
anti-poverty pro-
grams, etc.

35a. HOW MANY CLUBS OR ORGANIZATIONS, BESIDES THOSE
IN THE (PROJECT/CO-OP), DO YOU BELONG TO THAT
ARE IN THE NEIGHBORHOOD?

1 (ask b and c)......	1
2 " " " "	2
3 " " " "	3
4 " " " "	4
5 or more...........	5
None (skip to 36)....	0

b. WHAT ARE THE NAMES OF THESE ORGANIZATIONS?

List formal titles,
i.e., P.S. 129 PTA,
Church Action Club.

_____

_____

_____

_____

_____

c. DO YOU GO TO MEETINGS ABOUT ONCE A WEEK, 2 OR
3 TIMES A MONTH, ABOUT ONCE A MONTH, LESS OFTEN
THAN ONCE A MONTH OR ALMOST NEVER?

Once a week................	4
2 or 3 times a month.......	3
Once a month..............	2
Less often than a month....	1
Almost never..............	0

36a. I UNDERSTAND THAT PEOPLE WHO LIVE HERE ARE
ENCOURAGED TO WORK WITH OTHER TENANTS TO DECIDE
WHAT IS BEST FOR THE (PROJECT/CO-OP). IS THIS
TRUE?

Yes........	1
No.........	2

194

b. WOULD YOU EXPLAIN?

Probe   _____

Probe   _____

             _____

             _____

             _____

             _____

37a. ARE MOST OF THE PEOPLE WHO LIVE HERE NEGRO?

                    Yes (go to 38).............. 1
                    No (ask b).................. 2
                    Don't know (ask b).......... 3
                    Other _____

                    _____

                    _____

b. IS THE (PROJECT/CO-OP) WELL INTEGRATED?

                    Yes......................... 1
                    No.......................... 2
                    Other _____

                    _____

                    _____

38. HAVE YOU EVER OWNED A COOPERATIVE APARTMENT BEFORE?

                              Yes................. 1

                              No.................. 2

39. DO YOU FEEL THAT COOPERATIVE HOUSING OFFERS A BETTER
    WAY OF LIFE THAN RENTING AN APARTMENT?

                              Yes................. 1

                              No.................. 2

40. WHAT DO YOU FEEL IS DIFFERENT ABOUT OWNING A COOPERATIVE
    APARTMENT THAN RENTING AN APARTMENT?

Probe   _____

Probe   _____

Probe   _____

            _____

            _____

            _____

            _____

            _____

            _____

            _____

            _____

            _____

41. DO YOU FEEL THAT COOPERATIVE HOUSING IS A GOOD INVESTMENT
    FOR YOUR SAVINGS?

                              Yes............... 1

                              No................ 2

42a. MANY PEOPLE SAY THAT LIVING IN A COOPERATIVE IS LIKE OWNING YOUR OWN HOME. DO YOU AGREE WITH THIS?

Yes................. 1

No................. 2

b. WHY WOULD YOU SAY THAT?

Probe   _____

Probe   _____

Probe   _____

         _____

         _____

43a. DID YOU HAVE TO BORROW MONEY FOR THE DOWN PAYMENT?

Yes (ask b and c)......... 1

No (go to 44)............. 2

b. WERE YOU WORRIED ABOUT BORROWING MONEY FOR THIS PURPOSE?

Yes..................... 1

No..................... 2

c. WAS IT LESS THAN A QUARTER, ABOUT A HALF, ABOUT 3 QUARTERS, OR ALMOST THE FULL DOWN PAYMENT?

Less than a quarter....... 1

About a half............. 2

About three quarters...... 3

Almost full.............. 4

Other (specify) _____

_____

44a. WOULD YOU LIKE TO SEE SOME OF THE PROJECTS OR BUILDINGS
IN THIS NEIGHBORHOOD MADE INTO COOPERATIVES?

Yes.................. 1

No................... 2

b. WHY?

_____

_____

_____

_____

_____

_____

45a. WILL THERE BY ANY CHANGES IN POLICY FOR THE RESIDENTS
IN THE CO--OP NEXT YEAR?

Yes (ask b)................ 1

No........................ 2

b. WHAT WILL THE CHANGE(S) BE?

Raise in the rent........... 1

Other (specify) _____

_____

_____

_____

**Respondent's
comments
about rent
increase.**

_____

_____

_____

_____

Show card. Have
respondent tell
you number only.

46. WHICH OF THESE GROUPS COMES NEAREST TO YOUR TOTAL
FAMILY INCOME BEFORE TAXES. JUST TELL ME THE
NUMBER ON THE CARD.

<u>Per year</u>

Less than $3,000............ 2

$3,000 - $4,000............. 3

$4,000 - $5,000............. 4

$5,000 - $6,000............. 5

$6,000 - $7,000............. 6

$7,000 - $8,000............. 7

$8,000 - $9,000............. 8

$9,000 - $10,000............ 9

$10,000 and over............ 10

Refusal..................... X

To be filled out _after_ the interview.

1. Were the following visible in the living room?

	Yes	No
Carpeting	1	2
Framed pictures	1	2
Curtains	1	2
Photos of people	1	2
Real flowers - plants	1	2
Decorative pillows	1	2

2. Evaluate general cleanliness and housekeeping.

Good............... 3

Fair............... 2

Poor............... 1

3. Race

White............. 1

Negro............. 2

Puerto Rican....... 3

Other (specify)   _____

INTERVIEWER'S COMMENTS

_____

INTERVIEWER

38. IF YOU COULD CHOOSE, WOULD YOU PREFER TO RENT OR OWN
    YOUR OWN HOME?

    Rent.................. 1

    Own.................. 2

    Doesn't matter........ 3

39. WHAT KIND OF A PLACE WOULD YOU LIKE?

Probe   _____

Probe   _____

    _____

Read this if   40. DO YOU KNOW ANYTHING ABOUT COOPERATIVE APARTMENTS WHERE
respondent   YOU CAN BUY YOUR OWN APARTMENT?
doesn't seem to
understand. In   Yes.......... 1
a cooperative
each resident   No.......... 2
has a share in
owning and   41a. DO YOU KNOW OF ANY COOPERATIVE APARTMENTS AROUND HERE?
managing the
development and   Yes (go to 42)........ 1
can vote to
decide what is   No (ask b)............ 2
good for the
residents.   b. ARE YOU FAMILIAR WITH THE FRANKLIN PLAZA COOPERATIVE
They buy their   ON 106TH STREET?
apartment
with a down   Yes.................. 1
payment and
they can sell   No.................. 2
their apartment   42. DID YOU KNOW THAT THE PEOPLE AT FRANKLIN PLAZA OWN
if the want to   THEIR APARTMENTS?
move.

                            Yes.................. 1

                            No.................. 2

43a. IF YOU COULD CHOOSE WOULD YOU LIKE TO LIVE IN FRANKLIN
PLAZA?

Yes (ask c).......... 1

No (ask b).......... 2

b. WHY WOULDN'T YOU LIKE TO LIVE THERE?

Probe   _____

Probe   _____

                          _____

                          _____

                          _____

c. HAVE YOU EVER THOUGHT OF MOVING INTO FRANKLIN PLAZA?

Yes (ask d).......... 1

No (go to 44)........ 2

Check all
answers
that are
mentioned.

d. WHY HAVEN'T YOU MOVED THERE?

Too expensive........ ___

No money for down
payment.............. ___

Not a nice place..... ___

Different people
than I'm used to..... ___

Prefer renting....... ___

Would rather leave
East Harlem.......... ___

Other (specify)......

_____

_____

_____

44a. WOULD YOU LIKE TO BE ABLE TO OWN THE APARTMENT YOU ARE
     NOW LIVING IN IF THIS PROJECT WAS MADE A COOPERATIVE?

                              Yes (ask b).......... 1

                              No.................... 2

  b. IF THIS PROJECT WAS MADE A COOPERATIVE WOULD YOU BE
     WILLING TO BORROW MONEY TO BUY AN APARTMENT HERE?

                              Yes................... 1

                              No.................... 2

45a. DO YOU THINK THERE ARE DIFFERENCES WHEN PEOPLE RENT
     THEIR APARTMENTS LIKE HERE AT (JEFFERSON HOUSES/LEXINGTON
     HOUSES) THAN WHEN PEOPLE OWN THEIR APARTMENTS LIKE AT
     FRANKLIN PLAZA?

                              Yes................... 1

                              No.................... 2

  b. WHY WOULD YOU SAY THAT?

Probe   _____

Probe   _____

             _____

             _____

46. IF YOU HAD $2,000 OR WERE GIVEN $2,000 TOMORROW AND
     YOU HAD TO SPEND THE MONEY ON HOUSING, WHAT WOULD YOU
     DO?

                    Fix up this apartment....... 1

                    Move into another apartment
                    in this project............. 2

                    Buy an apartment in
                    Franklin Plaza.............. 3

                    Move out of East Harlem
                    to another apartment........ 4

                    Buy your own house.......... 5

                    Leave NYC altogether........ 6

                    Move to the country......... 7

                    Other _____

                    _____

203

47a. DO YOU THINK THAT LIVING IN THE PROJECT OFFERS YOU A
BETTER WAY OF LIFE THAN NOT LIVING IN IT?

Yes................... 1

No.................... 2

<u>Probe</u>   b. WHY? _____

<u>Probe</u>   _____

_____

48a. WILL THERE BE ANY CHANGES IN POLICY FOR THE TENANTS IN
THE PROJECT NEXT YEAR?

Yes (ask b).......... 1

No.................... 2

Do <u>not</u> read   b. WHAT WILL THE CHANGE(S) BE?
response.

Raise in the rent..... 1

Other (specify) _____

<u>Probe</u>   _____

_____

Show card.   49. WHICH OF THESE GROUPS COMES NEAREST TO YOUR TOTAL FAMILY
Have re-   INCOME BEFORE TAXES. JUST TELL ME THE NUMBER ON THE
spondent   CARD.
tell you
number only.

<u>Per year</u>

Less than $3,000............. 2

$3,000 - $4,000.............. 3

$4,000 - $5,000.............. 4

$5,000 - $6,000.............. 5

$6,000 - $7,000.............. 6

$7,000 - $8,000.............. 7

$8,000 - $9,000.............. 8

$9,000 - $10,000............. 9

$10,000 and over............. 10

Refusal...................... X

To be filled out _after_ the interview:

1. Were the following visible in the living room?

	Yes	No
Carpeting	1	2
Framed pictures	1	2
Curtains	1	2
Photos of people	1	2
Real flowers - plants	1	2
Decorative pillows	1	2

2. Evaluate general cleanliness and housekeeping.

Good.............. 3

Fair.............. 2

Poor.............. 1

3. Race

White............ 1

Negro............ 2

Puerto Rican...... 3

Other (specify) _____

INTERVIEWER'S COMMENTS

_____

INTERVIEWER

BIBLIOGRAPHY

BOOKS AND PAMPHLETS

Angell, Robert C. The Moral Integration of American
    Cities. Chicago: University of Chicago Press,
    1951.

Back, Kurt W. Slums, Projects and People. Durham,
    N.C.: Duke University Press, 1962.

Beyer, Glenn H. Housing: A Factual Analysis. New
    York: The Macmillan Company, 1958.

_____. Housing and Society. New York: The
    Macmillan Company, 1965.

Bogardus, Emory S. "Principles of Cooperation"
    Chicago: Cooperative League of the U.S.A.,
    1958. Part II.

Brown, Robert K. The Development of the Public
    Housing Program in the United States. Atlanta:
    Georgia State College of Business Administration,
    1960.

Chapin, F. Stuart. Experimental Designs in Sociolo-
    gical Research. New York: Harper Brothers,
    1955.

Citizens' Housing and Planning Council of New York,
    Inc. Directory of Large Scale Rental and
    Cooperative Housing. New York: Citizens
    Housing and Planning Council of New York, 1957.

Cohen, Lillian. Statistical Methods for Social
    Scientists. Englewood Cliffs, N.J.: Prentice-
    Hall, Inc., 1954.

Cooperative League of the U.S.A. "Plus Values in
    Cooperative Housing." Chicago: Cooperative
    League of the U.S.A. 1962.

Dean, John P. Home Ownership: Is it Sound? New
    York: Harper and Brothers, 1945.

Dobriner, William M., ed. The Suburban Community.
    New York: Putnam's Sons, 1958.

Festinger, Leon, Schachter, S. and Back, K. Social
    Pressures in Informal Groups. New York: Harper
    and Row, 1950.

Fisher, Ernest M. "A Study of Housing Programs and
    Policies." Washington, D.C.: Housing and Home
    Finance Agency, 1960.

Fisher, Robert M. Twenty Years of Public Housing.
    New York: Harper and Brothers, 1939.

Foley, Donald L. "Neighbors or Urbanites." Rochester,
    N.Y.: University of Rochester, Department of
    Sociology, 1952.

Foundation for Cooperative Housing. "Cooperative
    Development with Federal Assistance--The Founda-
    tion for Cooperative Housing." Housing--The
    Cooperative Way. Edited by Jerome Liblit.
    New York: Twayne Publishers, Inc., 1964.

Fox, Clara. "A Vertical Neighborhood in an Urban
    Renewal Community--Report of the Goddard Tower
    Cooperative." New York: National Federation
    of Settlements and Neighborhood Centers, 1969.

_____. "Volunteer Leadership in Cooperative
    Housing." New York: New York Play Schools
    Associations, 1960.

Freedman, Leonard. Public Housing: The Politics of
    Poverty, New York: Holt, Rinehart and Winston,
    Inc., 1969.

Fried, Marc. "Grieving for a Lost Home." The Urban

Condition. Edited by Leonard J. Duhl. New York: Basic Books, Inc., 1963.

Gans, Herbert J. _The Urban Villagers_. New York: The Free Press, 1962.

Goldblatt, Harold. "Residential Stability in an Integrated Middle Income Cooperative." (Report No. 15.) New York: City of New York Commission on Human Rights, 1964.

Gordon, Joan. "The Poor of Harlem: Social Functioning in the Underclass." New York: Office of the Mayor, Interdepartmental Neighborhood Service Center, 1965.

Hearings on H.R. 5840 and Related Bills. U.S. House of Representatives, Subcommittee on Housing of the Committee on Banking and Currency. (89th Cong., 1st sess.) Washington, D.C.: Government Printing Office, 1965. Part I.

Herman, James S. "Why Do You Live in an Apartment: A Study of a Sinister Trend in American Life." Detroit: Michigan Housing Association, 1931. Quoted in The President's Conference on Home Building and Home Ownership, _Housing and the Community--Home Repair and Remodelling_. Washington, D.C.: Government Printing Office, 1932.

Housing and Redevelopment Board. "Social and Economic Analysis of the East River Urban Renewal Area." New York: Housing and Redevelopment Board, March, 1965.

Lerner, D., and Lasswell, H. D., eds. _The Policy Sciences_. Stanford, Calif.: Stanford University Press, 1951.

Liblit, Jerome, ed. _Housing--The Cooperative Way_. New York: Twayne Publishers, Inc., 1964.

Linton, Ralph. _The Study of Man_. New York: Appleton-Century-Crofts, 1936.

Mayer, Albert. The Urgent Future. New York: McGraw-
     Hill Book Company, 1967.

Merton, Robert K. "The Social Psychology of Housing."
     Current Trends in Social Psychology. Edited
     by Wayne Dennis. Pittsburgh, Pa.: University
     of Pittsburgh Press, 1948.

Meyerson, Martin, et al. Housing, People, and Cities.
     New York: McGraw-Hill Book Company, Inc., 1962.

Miller, Delbert C. Handbook of Research Design and
     Social Measurement. New York: David McKay
     Company, Inc., 1964.

New York City Housing Authority. "1967 Guide to
     Housing Developments."

_____, Statistics Division. "Project Data:
     Characteristics of Tenants as of January 1, 1967."
     New York: New York City Housing Authority, 1967.

Nisbet, Robert. The Quest for Community. New York:
     Oxford University Press, 1953.

Percy, Charles H. "A New Dawn for Our Cities--The
     Homeownership Achievement Plan," Federal Role
     in Urban Affairs. (Senate Committee on Government
     Operations, 89th Congress, 2nd Session). Wash-
     ington, D.C.: Government Printing Office, 1966.
     Part 7.

President's Conference on Home Building and Home
     Ownership. Housing and The Community--Home
     Repair and Remodelling. Washington, D.C.:
     1932. Vol. IV.

Principles of Membership Education in Housing Coopera-
     tives. Proceedings of a seminar sponsored by
     the New York State Division of Housing and Community
     Renewal. Albany: New York State Division of
     Housing and Community Renewal, May 6, May 21
     and June 4, 1964.

Reach, Barbara. Social Aspects of Cooperative and

Non-Profit Housing: New and Rehabilitated. New
    York: Community Service Society of New York,
    1968.

Ross, Murray G. Community Organization: Theory
    and Principles. New York: Harper and Brothers,
    1955.

Ryan, Edward T. "Personal Identity in an Urban Slum."
    The Urban Condition. Edited by Leonard J. Duhl.
    New York: Basic Books, Inc., 1963.

Sanders, Irwin T. The Community. New York: The
    Ronald Press Company, 1958.

Schacter, Stanley, et al. "An Experimental Study of
    Cohesiveness and Productivity." Group Dynamics:
    Research and Theory. Edited by Dorwin Cartwright
    and A. Zander. Evanston, Ill.: Row, Peterson,
    1960.

Sexton, Patricia Cayo. Spanish Harlem. New York:
    Harper & Row, 1965.

Starr, Roger. The Living End: The City and Its
    Critics. New York: Coward-McCann, Inc., 1966.

Steiner, Jesse F. Community Organization. New York:
    The Century Company, 1925.

Vogel, Harold N. The Co-op Apartment. New York:
    Libra Publishers, Inc., 1960.

Voorhis, Jerry. American Cooperatives. New York:
    Harper Brothers, 1961

Wert, James E., Weidt, Charles O., and Ahmann, J.
    Stanley. Statistical Methods in Educational
    and Psychological Research. New York: Appleton-
    Century-Crofts, Inc., 1954.

Wheaton, William L. C., et al., eds. Urban Housing.
    New York: The Free Press, 1966.

Whyte, William H., Jr. The Organization Man. New

York: Simon and Schuster, 1956.

Wurster, Catherine Bauer. "The Dreary Deadlock of
    Public Housing." Urban Housing. Edited by
    William L. C. Wheaton et al. New York: The
    Free Press, 1966.

PERIODICALS

Angell, Robert C. "The Moral Integration of American
    Cities," American Journal of Sociology, LVII,
    Part 2 (July, 1951), pp. 119-120.

Axelrod, Morris. "Urban Structure and Social Parti-
    cipation," American Sociological Review, XXI
    (February, 1956), 13-18.

Barnett, William E. "Neighborhood Groups: An Informal
    System of Communication," Rural Sociology, XIX
    (September, 1952), 371-73.

Bell, Wendell and Boat, Marion B. "Urban Neighborhoods
    and Informal Social Relations," American Journal
    of Sociology, LXII (January, 1957), 391-98.

Caplow, Theodore. "Home Ownership and Location Pre-
    ferences in a Minnesota Sample," American Soci-
    ological Review, XIII (December, 1948), 725-30.

Caplow, Theodore, and Forman, Robert. "Neighborhood
    Interaction in a Homogeneous Community," American
    Sociological Review, XV (June, 1950), 357-66.

Chapin, F. Stuart. "Design for Social Experiments,"
    American Sociological Review, III (December,
    1938), 786-800.

_____ . "The Effects of Slum Clearance and Rehousing
    on Family and Community Relationships in Min-
    neapolis," American Journal of Sociology, XLIII
    (March, 1938), 744-63.

Fessler, Donald R. "The Development of a Scale for
    Measuring Community Solidarity," Rural Sociology,

XVII (April, 1952), 144-52.

Festinger, Leon. "Architecture and Group Membership,"
    Journal of Social Issues, VII, Nos. 1 and 2
    (1951).

Fried, Marc, and Gleicher, Peggy. "Some Sources of
    Residential Satisfaction in an Urban Slum,"
    Journal of American Institute of Planners, XXVII,
    No. 4 (November, 1961), 305-15.

Gans, Herbert J. "The Human Implications of Current
    Redevelopment and Relocation Planning," Journal
    of the American Institute of Planners, XXV
    (February, 1959), 15-25.

Goodman, Grace Ann. "Cooperative Housing for Middle-
    Income Families in the New York City Area."
    Mission through Housing. New York: Office of
    Church and Housing, United Presbyterian Church
    in the U.S.A. (1967).

Haar, Charles M. "Middle-Income Housing: The Coopera-
    tive Snare?," Land Economics, XXIX (November,
    1953), 289-94.

Hartman, Chester. "The Housing of Relocated Families,"
    Journal of the American Institute of Planners,
    XXX (November, 1964), 266-86.

Isaacs, Lewis M., Jr. "'To Buy or Not to Buy:
    That is the Question'. . . What's a Cooperative
    Apartment?," The Record (Association of the
    Bar of the City of New York), XIII, No. 4 (April,
    1958), 203-32.

Jonassen, Christian T. "Functional Unities in Eighty-
    Eight Community Systems," American Sociological
    Review, XXVI (June, 1961), 399-407.

Komarovsky, Mirra. "The Voluntary Association of
    Urban Dwellers," American Sociological Review,
    XI (December, 1946), 686-98.

Litwak, Eugene. "Reference Group Theory, Bureaucratic

Career, and Neighborhood Primary Group Cohesion,"
Sociometry, XXIII (March, 1960), 72-84.

Mather, William C. "Income and Social Participation,"
American Sociological Review, VI (June, 1941),
380-84.

Parsons, Talcott. "An Analytical Approach to the
Theory of Social Stratification," *American
Journal of Sociology*, V (May, 1940), 481-82.

Reiss, Albert J., Jr. "The Sociological Study of
Communities," *Rural Sociology*, XXIV, No. 2
(June, 1959), 118-30.

Schecter, George. "How To Work with Committees,"
Cooperative Housing Quarterly, I, No. 2 (Summer,
1963), 14-20.

Smith, Joel; Form, William H.; and Store, Gregory P.
"Local Intimacy in a Middle-Size City," *American
Journal of Sociology*, XV (November, 1954), 276-84.

Useem, Ruth Hill; Useem, John; and Gibson, Duane L.
"The Function of Neighboring for the Middle
Class Male," *Human Organization*, XIX (Summer,
1965), 68-76.

Wallin, Paul. "A Guttman Scale for Measuring Women's
Neighborliness," *American Journal of Sociology*,
LIX (November, 1953), 241-46.

Wirth, Louis. "Housing as a Field of Sociological
Research," *American Sociological Review*, XII
(April, 1947), 137-43.

Wurster, Catherine Bauer. "Social Questions in
Housing and Community Planning," *Journal of
Social Issues*, VII, Nos. 1 and 2 (1951), 1-33.

UNPUBLISHED MATERIALS

Boden, S.F., Association for Middle-Income Housing.
Letter to John Merli, President, Franklin Plaza

Apartments, Inc. (April 19, 1962).

Schneider, Martin, Public Relations Consultant,
     Victor Weingarten Company, Inc. Letter to Miss
     Mildred Zucker, Franklin Plaza Housing Company
     (September 6, 1963).

Donald G. Sullivan is Assistant Professor and Director of the Graduate Program in Urban Planning at Hunter College of the City University of New York. Professor Sullivan is also involved as a housing policy consultant to the New York City Housing and Development Administration with the RAND Corporation-- New York City Institute and the Hoboken, New Jersey, Model Cities Agency. Professor Sullivan holds the Ph.D. in housing and city planning and the Master of Regional Planning degree from Cornell University and a B.A. in political science from the City College of New York. The author is currently involved in studies dealing with city planning in working-class neighbor- hoods and the community development process in co- operative residential developments.